T0128391

The Life of Gampopa

To Khenpo Karthar Rinpoche, kind root lama; Khenpo Könchog Gyaltsen Rinpoche, spiritual friend and master; and to Adam Mackenzie Stewart and Gabriel Drews Stewart, my beloved sons.

The Life of Gampopa

by
Jampa Mackenzie Stewart

Introduction by
Lobsang P. Lhalungpa

Snow Lion
Boston & London

Snow Lion
An imprint of Shambhala Publications, Inc.
Horticultural Hall
300 Massachusetts Avenue
Boston, Massachusetts 02115
www.shambhala.com

Second Edition

Printed in the United States of America

⊗This edition is printed on acid-free paper that meets the
American National Standards Institute Z39.48 Standard.
♻Shambhala Publications makes every effort to print on recycled
paper. For more information please visit www.shambhala.com.
Distributed in the United States by Penguin Random House LLC
and in Canada by Random House of Canada Ltd

The Library of Congress catalogues the previous edition of this book as follows:
Stewart, Jampa Mackenzie, 1951–
The life of Gampopa: the incomparable Dharma Lord of Tibet / by Jampa
Mackenzie Stewart.
p. cm.
Includes bibliographical references and index.
ISBN 978-1-55939-038-5 (1st edition)
ISBN 978-1-55939-214-3 (2nd edition)
1. Sgam-po-pa, 1079–1153. 2. Bka'-rgyud-pa lamas—China—Tibet—
Biography. I. Title.
BQ7950.S437S74 1994
294.3'923'092—dc20
[B] 94-39646
CIP

Contents

Preface

Biographies of saints are written to inspire us. They depict the struggles and ultimate victory of people who have traveled the path before us. Good biographies give us role models for our own spiritual work, and incite us to greater efforts than would the mere words of a dissertation or sermon. They show us that it is the practical application of the practice—the actions of such saints—that are the teachings, and not just their words.

Several years ago my root lama, Venerable Khenpo Karthar Rinpoche, gave a teaching on the lives of the Kagyu forefathers, at Karma Triyana Dharmachakra in Woodstock, New York. This was the first time that I had heard the story of Gampopa's life. I was greatly moved by the fascinating tale of this yogi-monk who inherited the robe and bowl of the great Milarepa, and who gathered around him an unprecedented 51,600 monks and over 500 *yogi* disciples. These included the first Karmapa and the renowned Phagmo Drupa. Since Gampopa was the father of all the Kagyupa lineages, known as the Four Great and Eight Younger Lineages (which are described in the appendix by Lobsang Lhalungpa), I felt that his story deserved a wider audience.

Over the last century biographies of other forefathers in the Kagyu lineage have been translated and published: Naropa, Marpa, the Karmapas, and recently, Tilopa. It therefore seemed strange to me that a complete biography of Gampopa had not been published in English, and even more strange because Gampopa's writings were some of the earliest works to be translated from the Tibetan.

Walter Yeeling Evans-Wentz and Lama Kazi Dawa Samdup translated Gampopa's *Supreme Path: The Rosary of Precious Gems* in *Tibetan*

Yoga and Secret Doctrines, one of the first Tibetan Buddhist teachings offered in English as serious yogic practice for personal transformation. However, this was a short work, well hidden in the midst of the more exciting and exotic practices of the *Six Yogas of Naropa,* the *Chod* practice, and the *Yoga of the Great Symbol* (the Four Yogas of *Mahamudra.*) Although I spent many hours perusing that book, it was years later that I discovered in a casual conversation that *The Rosary of Precious Gems* was written by the great Gampopa.

Similarly, a short yet excellent biography of Gampopa is presented by Garma C. C. Chang in Volume II of *The Hundred Thousand Songs of Milarepa.* Yet, as Milarepa himself is the focal point of that book, Gampopa's life story is naturally eclipsed by the stories of his *guru.*

The work by which Gampopa's name is perhaps best known in the West is Herbert V. Guenther's translation of Gampopa's great work, *The Jewel Ornament of Liberation.* Therein Gampopa presents a brilliant outline of the Stages of the Path to Enlightenment (*Lam Rim*) in the traditional *Kadampa* fashion, combined with the Mahamudra lineage view inherited from his guru, Milarepa. However, in this work the translator provides only one scant page of details on the life of Gampopa.

Other partial accounts of Gampopa's life story have been translated into English, to which I am greatly indebted in preparing my own rendering. Venerable Khenpo Könchog Gyaltsen Rinpoche included a brief but excellent biography of Gampopa in his book, *Prayer Flags: The Spiritual Songs of Lord Jigten Sumgon.* He also included a longer biography in his work, *The Great Kagyu Masters: The Golden Lineage Treasury* (edited by Victoria Huckenpahler), from which I drew much valuable material, in particular the miraculous stories included in chapter eighteen of this book. *The Rain of Wisdom,* translated by the Nalanda Translation Committee under the direction of the late Chogyam Trungpa Rinpoche, included "The Life and Songs of Lord Gampopa" and "Lord Gampopa's Song of Response to the Three Men of Kham" among the songs of the great Kagyu lineage masters. As before, Gampopa's story lies hidden among many others in each of these versions. A very short segment on Gampopa's life also appears in the recent work, *A Garland of Gold: The Early Kagyu Masters in India and Tibet* by Jampa Thaye. I also found two short stories about Gampopa in *Tantric Practice in Nyingma* by Khetsun Sangpo Rinbochay, translated and edited by Jeffrey Hopkins, a commentary on Paltrul

Rinpoche's *Kunzang Lamay Zhalung*, which are included in chapter eighteen. I am also deeply indebted to Khenpo Karthar Rinpoche for his oral transmission on the life of Gampopa.

Even in Tibetan, I know of no single complete biography of Gampopa's life. Of the versions I have mentioned, some included great detail on the early part of Gampopa's life but little or nothing about his later life. In other versions the reverse was true. Areas that would be covered in a single sentence in one version receive several pages in another. It has been my intention to present as complete, accurate and detailed an account of Gampopa's life as possible. To prepare such a comprehensive English biography I have researched, compiled, translated, and edited many different sources.

In most of these sources the stories were in complete agreement, but in others the accounts were puzzlingly divergent. For example: *Prayer Flags* gives Gampopa's mother's name as Ngalsa; in the *Hundred Thousand Songs of Milarepa* his father had two wives, and it is unclear whether Yunlaza or Sangden Dranma was his actual mother; while Guenther, in *The Jewel Ornament of Liberation*, gives Gampopa's mother's name as Somoza Chelcam! Other differences in each account concerned the age at which Gampopa married, the duration of his marriage before his wife's death, and where and with whom he took monastic ordination.

In all these cases I sought to present the version or combination of versions that seemed the most logical and consistent and allowed the story to flow best. For I believe that a story should be told well, and I have sought to fulfill the role of storyteller, and not just translator and editor. There are, for example, many tellings of the life and legend of the Buddha. Each has its own color and flavor, in accordance with the intuitions and talents of the particular storyteller.

To aid me in these efforts I received the Guru Yoga empowerment of Gampopa from both Venerable Khenpo Karthar Rinpoche and His Eminence Jamgon Kongtrul Rinpoche, whose blessings have helped guide me to an inner sense of the man Gampopa. These blessings have been especially helpful in dealing with those periods in Gampopa's life in which details were sparse or disparate in the existing accounts.

In fact, this work is an interdependent co-arising, resulting from the efforts of many people. I particularly wish to thank the following individuals: Venerable Khenpo Karthar Rinpoche, my root lama, for his kindness to me, which can never be repaid, and for his teachings

on the Kagyu forefathers, which inspired me to write this story of
Gampopa; Venerable Khenpo Könchog Gyaltsen, for sending me the
short biography of Gampopa that subsequently appeared in *Prayer
Flags*, for apprising me of the presence of a biography of Gampopa
hidden within the recesses of the *Hundred Thousand Songs of Milarepa*,
for permission to use portions of his translations from *Prayer Flags*
and *The Great Kagyu Masters*, for his encouragement, and for his reverence for the undying presence of the man, Gampopa; the late Jamgon
Kongtrul Rinpoche, for his initiation and praise of the great Dharma
Lord Gampopa—may the world be graced with his swift rebirth;
Lobsang P. Lhalungpa for his essay included herein, his generous assistance in editing the manuscript, his patience in answering my many
questions about Tibet, his clarification of Gampopa's unique contributions to the Mahamudra, and for his unending supply of delicious
tea and cookies while we painstakingly reviewed the manuscript.

In addition to these precious teachers, I want to express my appre-
ciation to the following people for their invaluable contributions: Kim-
berly Baldt, for her assistance with data entry, her comments and criticism of the evolving manuscript, her proofreading, and her encouragement and support throughout every phase of this project; Eva van
Dam for agreeing to grace this story with her excellent and inspiring
art work; Jonathan Landaw, for his thorough editing and constructive
comments on the entire finished manuscript, his compassionate criticism and wholehearted encouragement, and the generous contribution of his valuable time to this project; Sarah Harding, for her review
and comments on the early manuscript and for her loan of Tibetan
manuscripts; Claudia Drews, for her caring for our children while I
worked on this book; Lynnette Brooks for her generous assistance
in preparing the index; Jeffrey Cox and Sidney Piburn of Snow Lion
Publications, for their patient support and encouragement.

> Through the merit of these combined efforts, and through the
>   blessings of you, kind Lord Gampopa,
> May we, and all sentient beings, be able to cut the continuum of
>   self-grasping,
> May we be able to train in love, compassion and the mind of
>   enlightenment,
> May you transform us by your inspiring strength to reach the
>   unsurpassable Mahamudra union swiftly through the paths.

I am sure that there will be some errors in this rendering of the life
of Gampopa, for which I take full responsibility. Nonetheless, I pray

that the brilliant light of the Dharma Lord Gampopa will blaze through these simple words and inspire all of you who read this book.

In the words of Gampopa:

> Grant your blessings
> so that my mind may be one with the Dharma.
>
> Grant your blessings
> so that the Dharma may become the path.
>
> Grant your blessings
> so that by following the path, confusion may be clarified.
>
> Grant your blessings
> so that confusion may dawn as wisdom.

Introduction

by Lobsang P. Lhalungpa

Gampopa Sonam Rinchen (1079-1153 C.E.) evokes reverence among Tibetans of all backgrounds and religious affinities. Gampopa was the founder of the Dakpo Kagyupa Order, and thus the spiritual father of most Kagyupa branches established by his disciples. While Marpa, Milarepa, and Gampopa were all widely recognized as the three original Tibetan masters of the Kagyupa tradition, the rapid spread of Kagyupa monasteries, teachings, and adherents was essentially due to Gampopa's preeminence in Buddhist teachings and attainment.

Like many great teachers, Gampopa had an eclectic training. In his younger years Gampopa married and practiced medicine. During early adulthood, when his wife and children suddenly died during an epidemic, he felt a strong urge to renounce the worldly life and pursue religious studies. He entered a Kadampa monastery and became a fully ordained monk. He studied the teachings of the *Three Vehicles* under many Kadampa masters in the Ü region of Tibet.

The Kadampa order was established under the guidance of the great Indian teacher, Dipankara Atisha, during the eleventh century, the period of the Buddhist renaissance in Tibet. Gampopa was widely regarded as belonging to the highest rank of *lamas*, reverentially called "Khedrup Nyidan"—one who has achieved both scholarship and self-realization. By virtue of his diligence, moral strength, and intellectual sensitivity he became a very accomplished scholar and a compassionate teacher.

Then he felt a strong urge to seek out the renowned Milarepa in one of his many mountain caves, high up in the Jomo Langmo (Mt. Everest) ranges. The climax of Gampopa's life was his meeting with Milarepa, whose fame was then reverberating throughout Tibet. While Gampopa was overwhelmed with joy at meeting Milarepa, Milarepa also felt great pleasure in meeting Gampopa. Earlier, Milarepa had experienced a prophetic vision about the qualities and destiny of his would-be disciple.

There is some similarity between the way Gampopa and Naropa found fulfillment of their cherished aspirations through their respective teachers. Both Gampopa and Naropa were highly accomplished scholars and Dharma practitioners with stable and secure positions. Naropa was the abbot of the famed Nalanda University in India, while Gampopa was a lineage holder of the Kadampa order. They both left the comfort of their positions to follow wild mahasiddha yogis of the Mahamudra lineage, under whose guidance they attained the full fruition of *Buddhahood*. But where Tilopa succeeded with Naropa through his seemingly crazy and cruel treatment, Milarepa brought Gampopa to fruition through respect and kindness. Though endowed with a different personality and character from that of his revered teacher, Gampopa nevertheless embodied the full wisdom of Marpa's and Milarepa's attainment.

Milarepa ultimately chose Gampopa over his long-time disciple, Rechung, to be the supreme upholder of the entire Kagyupa teachings. Milarepa himself proclaimed Gampopa to be a great *bodhisattva*. He entrusted Gampopa with the task of guiding the Kagyupa Order, thus realizing the prophecy of Buddha that a reincarnation of the Bodhisattva Chandra Prabha Kumara would emerge as a young physician from south Tibet and would illuminate the "Land of the Snowy Mountains" with his teachings.

The Life of Gampopa

Tibetan, Sanskrit, and other technical terms appear in italics on their first occurrence. Explanations of these terms can be found in the glossary.

1 The Prophecies

Among all the disciples of Jetsun Milarepa, lord of yogis, the foremost was the supremely exalted Dharma Lord Gampopa. Many prophecies foretold Gampopa's appearance in Tibet, the Land of Snows.

Milarepa himself had numerous dreams and visions predicting the coming of Gampopa. One day, while Milarepa was still a disciple, sitting at the feet of his great *vajra* master, Marpa the Translator, Mila and the other disciples requested, "Precious Guru, since you are getting old now, please prophesy how the ear-whispered teachings of the Kagyu will spread in the future."

Marpa replied, "As a descendent of the great teacher Naropa's lineage, I do have the power to prophesy through dreams. So, my heart-son disciples, go now and remember your dreams tonight, so that I might predict the future growth of my spiritual lineage."

After practicing dream yoga, the disciples returned and related their dreams to Marpa. Even though the other disciples had good dreams, they were of no prophetic consequence. However, Milarepa had a vivid dream, which he offered to the guru in song:

> Last night I dreamed a dream.
> I share its story with the lama,
> Please listen while I tell of it.

> In the vast northern region of the world,
> I dreamt there was a majestic snow-clad mountain.
> I dreamt its snowy summit touched the sky.
> I dreamt its peak was circled by the sun and moon.
> I dreamt their light rays filled the sky.
> I dreamt its base covered the entire earth.
> I dreamt the rivers descended in the four directions.

I dreamt their waters satisfied all beings.
I dreamt the rivers flowed into the ocean.
I dreamt on the shores myriad flowers bloomed.

Mila then sang that in each of the four directions a massive pillar stood. Atop each pillar sat an animal, and each animal was engaged in a different activity. Of the northern pillar, Milarepa sang the following verse:

Northward, I dreamt that a great pillar stood.
I dreamt a fearless vulture perched upon the pillar's top.
I dreamt the vulture's wings were fully spread.
I dreamt she made a nest among the rocks.
I dreamt she gave birth to a young one.
I dreamt that from this one the sky was filled with birds.
I dreamt the vulture's eyes gazed upward.
I dreamt she soared through the vast expanse of space.
Thus I relate to you, Guru, Buddha of the three times.

I took this as a happy omen
And rejoiced at its good fortune.
Please tell me now its inner meaning.

Thus Milarepa sang. Marpa was extremely pleased, and exclaimed, "This is an excellent dream!" He asked his wife Dakmema to prepare a sacred feast (*ganachakra*) in celebration.

When the preparations were complete and the heart-son disciples had assembled, the guru announced, "Mila Vajra Victory Banner[1] has had a marvelous dream!"

The disciples were excited, and supplicated Marpa to interpret the dream and reveal what the signs foretold. In the melody of the kingly voice, Marpa sang this *doha* song in reply:

Lord Buddha of the three times and *refuge* of beings,
Master Naropa, I prostrate at your feet.
All you disciples seated here at this place,
The astonishing omens that appear in this dream
Foretell a wondrous future!
Listen now as I, your old father, reveal them to you.

The northern region of the world is Tibet,
A sign that the Buddha's teachings will flourish here.
The snow-clad mountain rising above it
Is the old father, Marpa the Translator,
And all the Kagyu teachings.
The snowy peak touching the sky

Is the unsurpassable view.
The sun and moon circling around its peak
Are meditation, radiating wisdom and compassion.
The light rays filling up the skies
Are compassion, dispelling the darkness of ignorance.
Its base covering the entire earth
Is the vast expanse of the Buddha's activity on earth.
The four rivers descending in the four directions
Are the oral instructions of the *four initiations* that ripen and liberate.
Their waters quenching the thirst of all beings
Means that all disciples will be ripened and free.
The rivers flowing into the ocean
Is a sign of the meeting of *mother and son luminosities*.
The many flowers blooming along the shore
Are the flawless experiences of fruition.

Marpa then revealed in song that the four pillars each represented one of his heart-son disciples and his future accomplishments. Of the northern pillar, Marpa sang:

The great pillar rising to the North
Is Milarepa of Gungthang.
The fearless vulture perched upon the top
Is a symbol of his vulture-like nature.[2]
The vulture's wings fully spread
Means he has the full transmission of the ear-whispered oral
    teachings.
Its nest among the rocks
Means that his life-force will be harder than rock.
The vulture giving birth to a young one
Is a sign that one without equal will come.
The flock of young birds filling the sky
Is a sign that from this one the Kagyu teachings will spread.
Her eyes gazing upward
Is a sign that he will bid farewell to *samsara*.
The vulture soaring through the vast heart of space
Is his arrival in the realm of liberation.

Thus says this old father:
In the future, the Practice Lineage will gloriously flourish!

In this way Marpa prophesied from Milarepa's "Dream of the Four Pillars" that the young vulture chick symbolized a great disciple who would come to Milarepa from the north, one who would cause the Kagyu lineage to proliferate. Gampopa did indeed come to Milarepa from the north as foretold, became the heart-son of Milarepa, and was without peer in all of Tibet for his vast accomplishments and his spreading of the doctrine.

Milarepa later had another dream-vision, wherein the meditation deity *Vajrayogini* appeared and told him that he would have one disciple like the sun, another like the moon, and twenty-five accomplished disciples who would shine like stars among men. Of these illustrious disciples, Gampopa would be like the sun, the brightest light, and the foremost of all.

Gampopa had been a bodhisattva in many previous lifetimes, prior to the time of Buddha Shakyamuni, the fourth Buddha. Even before the time of the third Buddha, Dipankara Buddha, he served and benefitted many beings under the name of Lotus Guru. During the time of the third Buddha, he incarnated as the bodhisattva Beautiful Moon Flower.

The perfect Buddha, Shakyamuni himself, also prophesied the coming of Gampopa in *The Sutra of the King of Meditative Concentration* (*Samadhi-raja Sutra*) and elsewhere. For instance, in *The Lotus of Great Compassion Sutra* (*Mahakaruna-pundarika Sutra*), the Buddha said,

> Ananda! In the future, after my passing, a monk called "The Physician" will appear in the north. He rendered outstanding service to the previous Buddha, after having served hundreds of thousands of Buddhas in his previous lives. He is well grounded in virtues and the great altruistic motivation, and has entered the stainless path of the Great Vehicle for the benefit and happiness of countless sentient beings.
>
> He will appear as a well-informed man, highly versed in the scriptures of the bodhisattva doctrine. He will speak the word of the Great Vehicle and demonstrate the *Mahayana* teachings flawlessly and perfectly.

During the time of Buddha Shakyamuni, Gampopa was his student, a bodhisattva benefiting beings under the name of *New Moonlight Healer*. New Moonlight Healer was the son of a wealthy householder in Rajagraha. As his name suggests, he was not only a bodhisattva, but a wonderful and gifted physician as well. He healed the sick by giving them herbal medicine, but so powerful was the blessing of his being, that sometimes, when people merely heard his name, or when he simply touched the place of affliction, his patients were healed.

At one time, when Shakyamuni Buddha was turning the wheel of the Dharma at Vulture's Peak near Rajagraha, New Moonlight Healer invited the Buddha, along with the other bodhisattvas and disciples, to his home. When the Buddha and his entourage arrived, New Moonlight Healer supplicated the Blessed One to give a teaching. In response, Lord Buddha gave the teaching that became known as the *Samadhiraja Sutra*. After revealing this teaching, the Buddha asked who, of all his students present, would come forward as volunteers to spread the teaching of this *sutra*. Among all the accomplished students and bodhisattvas, New Moonlight Healer stood up and promised to spread the sutra and to make its message available to future beings.

After New Moonlight Healer made this vow, the Buddha promised him that in the future, when New Moonlight Healer spread the *Samadhi-raja Sutra*, he himself, Shakyamuni Buddha, would appear to help New Moonlight Healer establish these teachings firmly.

And so, in order to spread the teachings, New Moonlight Healer appeared in Tibet, the snow country of the north. He became known as Gampopa *Dakpo Lhaje*, and his fame spread throughout the land. He was a great bodhisattva, one who reached the tenth and final stage of the *bodhisattva path*, and had realized it with direct insight. Jetsun Milarepa foresaw Gampopa's arrival in his meditation. He blessed Gampopa with the grace of meditative concentration, and drew Gampopa to him with his mind power. Thus the sun-like Gampopa dawned upon the Buddhist religion in Tibet, and brought countless sentient beings to realization.

2 Gampopa the Layman

The Lord Gampopa took rebirth in the Sewa Valley of Nyel, in central Tibet, during the year of the Earth Sheep, 1079 C.E. His father was a physician named Wutso Gabar Gyalpo. Wutso Gabar Gyalpo had two wives, Yunlaza and Sangdan Dranma. Each of the wives gave birth to a son, and Gampopa was the eldest of the two. His parents named him Dunpa Dharma Drak.

While still a child, Gampopa displayed many splendid qualities. His father, being wise in worldly affairs, educated him well, so that he became skilled in speech and in medical consultation. He showed great interest in many subjects, and because of his enthusiasm, devotion, and openness, he was acknowledged as a great physician and scholar by the time he was sixteen, and had already received many tantric teachings of the Nyingmapa lineage from various gurus. Some of the transmissions bestowed upon young Gampopa were The Basic Tantra of *Guhyasamaja*, Heruka Gyalpo, the *Shi Tro*, and The Tantra of the Great Merciful Net Holder. He also mastered the eight branches of medical science, under the careful guidance of his father.

At the age of twenty-two he married the noble sister of Dharma Ö, the powerful local king. She had all the admirable qualities of a lady: she was gentle, graceful, well-mannered, strong, beautiful, faithful, melodious in speech, and very intelligent.

Gampopa and his wife lived together in happiness. Over time they had two children, a son and a daughter.

Then, several years after their marriage, an epidemic broke out in the region. As a physician, Gampopa worked day and night trying to heal the many victims of this terrible pestilence. Yet the plague claimed life after life.

One evening, Gampopa returned home to find that his only young son had died of the epidemic disease. The next morning, Gampopa carried the child's body in his arms to the cemetery, and there said many prayers for the boy's fortunate rebirth. He walked home alone.

When he arrived home, he found that his only daughter had also fallen sick with the same illness. Several days later she too was dead. Once again, Gampopa walked to the charnel grounds, this time carrying his daughter's limp little body in his arms. There, as he had done for his son, he said many prayers for her fortunate rebirth. Once again he walked home alone, a father no more.

A few days later, his wife fell ill. Gampopa tried every kind of medical treatment he knew to cure her. He repeated prayer after prayer, he performed healing sacraments and ceremonies, he used every medical tool and herb he had ever learned. All these were in vain, her sickness worsened, and she suffered much pain.

Yet, despite the seemingly endless torment she endured, she tried desperately to hold onto her life. Gampopa could do nothing but keep her company in her agony. Hour after hour, day after day, he sat beside her bed and recited the holy sutras aloud, in an effort to offer her some comfort.

After several days the thought occurred to him, "She is trying so hard to cling to life through this horrible ordeal. Why won't she just let herself die peacefully? Why is she fighting so hard? She must be deeply attached to something."

Then he said to her, "Beings who do not understand the true futile nature of samsara, end up feeling overburdened and exhausted. They feel compelled to linger in samsara, and so they are miserable and pitiable. I feel truly sorry for those unenlightened people who have such intense attachment to their dreamlike consorts and relatives.

"My love, my wife, you could let yourself die peacefully. You don't have to go through this prolonged ordeal. Yet you seem to be clinging to something, or to someone.

"If it is the house and the land that you cannot bear to leave, I'll offer them to the monks. If it is our jewels that you cannot give up, I'll give them to the priests and the poor. What else is there that you cannot let go of?

"We met in this life due to our mutual vows in previous lifetimes, but because of your bad *karma*, you have caught this disease. I have tried everything to help, but have only prolonged your suffering. This has been a painful lesson for me. I have decided that no matter whether you live or die, I will devote the rest of my life to the Dharma."

His wife, so weak that she was barely able to look at him, or raise her voice to speak, confessed to him, "I am now about to die. I have no attachment to our possessions. I am not attached to our wealth. I am not attached to fame. But I am very attached to you!

"You are young, and very handsome. Now I am dying, and when I am dead, you will marry a beautiful woman and forget me! I will send for my brother, Dharma Ö, to prevent you from being seduced by beautiful women!

"Besides, you can see from this that family life in samsara is without true happiness, as you have said. Oh, my dear husband, my physician, I hope that you will now devote your body and soul completely to the Dharma."

Gampopa replied softly, "Even if you were to recover from this disease, we cannot stay together forever. If you die, I will become a monk. Do you want me to swear it before you?"

His wife answered, "I know that you are a man who will never go back on your word, but to set my heart completely at rest, it would make me happy if you did take an oath before me."

Gampopa then called in his uncle, Palso, to bear witness. He placed a holy sutra, written in golden words, upon his head, and took the oath to become a monk and devote his life to the Dharma.

After seeing this, Gampopa's dear wife grasped her husband's hand and gazed into his eyes. Her heart now at ease, she sighed peacefully, and breathed no more.

Deeply saddened by the loss of his entire family, Gampopa divided his property into three parts, using one part to pay for his wife's funeral and offerings, another for meritorious charities, and the third to provide for learning and practicing the Dharma. He then cremated his wife's corpse and made a number of *tsa tsa*, clay Buddha images, with her ashes and bones. He built a *stupa* in her memory, which later became very famous. The people called it Jomo Chorten, Stupa of the Wife. It can still be seen in the region of Nyel.

Thus Gampopa Dakpo Lhaje, the physician from Dakpo, learned the lesson of impermanence and death. As a result of this bitter teaching on the unsatisfactory nature of samsara, the great Gampopa chose to renounce the world, to pursue no longer the *eight worldly dharmas*. Thus he was able to benefit countless beings through his diligent practice of the Dharma, with the merit of his attainment shining across the centuries even up to the present day.

3 Gampopa the Monk

After the funeral, Gampopa felt very much relieved to have wound up his worldly affairs. He thought, "Now it is time for me to practice Dharma." So he went alone to a place called Nyi Thong and meditated there.

Meanwhile, Gampopa's uncle Palso was feeling concerned about him. Uncle Palso thought, "My poor nephew must be heartbroken after the loss of his wife. He loved her so much. I should go to see if I can console him." So Uncle Palso gathered much wine and meat, and went to see Gampopa to offer him some good cheer.

Gampopa had just finished his afternoon meditation session when Palso arrived. They exchanged warm greetings, Gampopa invited his uncle in, and they began to enjoy the wine and meat together.

Palso had expected to find his nephew deep in mourning, as any devoted Tibetan husband would be after such a loss—this was the tradition. But Gampopa's vow to turn his whole life toward the Dharma had rekindled in him the karmic fire of countless lifetimes as a bodhisattva. He found that meditation suited him. Even in this short time of solitary retreat, he had already accomplished great calmness of mind.

Poor Palso did not know what to make of it. This was not ordinary behavior. It did not make sense to him that his nephew seemed so peaceful, indeed almost radiant, after such a loss. It was unsettling to Palso.

At one point during their conversation, Gampopa said to his uncle, "Since my wife passed away, I have been feeling very much at ease and happy."

This remark made Uncle Palso furious. "Where could you find a woman as good as your departed wife?" he cried indignantly. "If

Dharma Ö heard of this, he would say that you were breaking your marriage vows!"

With this, in his rage, he grabbed a handful of dust and threw it in Gampopa's face.

Gampopa did not retaliate. He merely wiped the dust from his eyes and replied, "My dear uncle, have you forgotten the oath I made before my wife on her deathbed, with you as my witness? Am I not practicing the Dharma as I promised?"

Palso's anger melted. The simple truth of Gampopa's words struck the core of his being. "Nephew, you are right," he said. "Though I have grown old, wrinkled, and gray, I have no insight or wisdom whatsoever. I seldom even think of the Dharma, let alone practice it! I really feel very ashamed of myself. Prosper in your Dharma practice, my nephew. I will look after your land and property."

After Uncle Palso's visit, Gampopa decided that he needed more instruction in the holy Dharma if he was going to truly master the way of the Buddha. He also wished to fulfill his promise to become a monk. So, unbeknownst to his relatives, he packed a few belongings, left his solitary retreat place at Nyi Thong, and made the journey to the famous Kadampa stronghold, Poto Monastery in the region of Phan Yu, north of Lhasa.

Upon arriving, he sought audience with the guru there, Lama Potowa Rinchensel. Gampopa was shown into the abbot's quarters. He bowed respectfully upon entering, and offered the traditional white scarf of greeting. Then Gampopa spoke:

"*Khenpo Rinpoche*, I am a native of Nyel. I have come here to devote my life to the Dharma. I ask you to please open the door for me, be my guide, and keep me here awhile."

The abbot Potowa answered, "I have no alms to give you. If you want to learn the Dharma here, you must provide your own food and clothing."

Gampopa thought to himself, "If I had the means to do that, I would not have asked. According to the Tantra of Guhyasamaja, a guru should have four kinds of compassion to benefit sentient beings: constant compassion, spontaneous compassion, compassion of granting blessings and prayers, and the compassion of guiding the disciples according to their needs. Only in this way can a guru help sentient beings. This lama seems to have little compassion. I doubt that my karma is linked with his. I cannot venerate him."

And so Gampopa left the Poto Monastery, journeyed back to Nyel, and gathered sixteen ounces of gold to provide the means for studying the Dharma. Then he traveled back to Phan Yu, but this time went instead to the Gyachakri or "Iron Wall" Monastery. There he was accepted, and shortly thereafter, at the age of twenty-six, he received full monastic ordination as a *bhikshu* under Lama Gyachilwa, and was given the name Sonam Rinchen, meaning Precious Merit.

From Shawa Lingpa and Chadulwa Dzinpa, the new monk Sonam Rinchen received the teaching of the *Six Treatises of the Kadampa*, the *Mahayana Sutralankara*, the *Abhisamayalankara*, the *Abhidharmakosha*, and others. All these teachings he mastered.

In Maryul, he received the *empowerments* of *Chakrasamvara* and the oral instructions on meditation from the great Kadampa Geshe Maryul Loden Sherab. From this teacher he received the tantric transmissions of *Hevajra*, Guhyasamaja and others.

He then journeyed to central Tibet, where, under the guidance of the renowned Kadampa masters Geshe Chadulwa Dzinpa, Geshe Gyachakri Gangkawa, Gyayon Dak and Geshe Nyugrumpa, he studied and learned all of the teachings of Lord Atisha, the father of the Kadampa lineage.

At this point, Sonam Rinchen thought, "Now I must practice these teachings." With that aim, he built a small house for himself close to the monastery, and with his needs taken care of from the farm land that he owned, he meditated in Gyachakri.

Sonam Rinchen was a man whose wisdom and compassion were great, and whose clinging and desire were small, whose diligence and faith toward the Dharma were prodigious, and whose apathy and laziness were negligible. He studied the Dharma by day, and meditated devotedly by night. He circumambulated stupas and other holy places, and performed many other meritorious acts. Due to his great compassion and purity, insects would not bite him. He could live without food comfortably for five or six days, and his body would always feel blissful. He could remain absorbed in *samadhi* for many days, and all gross forms of desire, aversion and ignorance subsided in him. As prophesied in the *Golden Light Sutra* (*Suvarna-prabhasottama-sutra*), all the signs preceding achievement of the tenth and final stage of a bodhisattva's enlightenment appeared unmistakably in his dreams. Thus did his understanding of both the theory and practice of the Buddha's teachings become fully ripened.

4 The Call of the Guru

Some time later, Gampopa Sonam Rinchen had a strange vision. In this vision there appeared before him a green yogi dressed all in rags. The yogi placed one hand upon Gampopa's head, wet a finger with spit, and flicked it in Gampopa's face.

Gampopa immediately felt his meditative concentration growing stronger and deeper. He experienced a penetrating understanding of reality. Filled with bliss, his mind became clearer and more alert than ever before. His entire being felt so light that it seemed he could almost fly. The apparition soon faded, but the lucidity remained.

Later he told some monks in the town about his vision and experience. The monks admonished Gampopa. They said to him, "You were ordained a bhikshu. Until now, you have been observing the pure precepts flawlessly. If you start dreaming of yogis and such you will run into trouble, because that type of dream is conjured up by the demon *Beghar*.

"You had better go to your teacher and ask him to give you the oral transmission for the *mantra* of the Immovable White *Achala*—the remover of all obstacles. You should arrange to have a special blessing *puja* done on your behalf by the monks in the assembly. You should also receive the oral transmission blessing of One Hundred *Torma* Offerings, to bless, protect, and purify you. Then, maybe the demon Beghar will be pacified and these obstacles can be avoided."

Gampopa promptly followed their advice and received the One Hundred Torma Blessings, yet the vision of the yogi continued to appear even more often than before.

Meanwhile, in the Happy Sunlit Cave of Drakmar Potho, Jetsun Milarepa was turning the wheel of the Dharma of both the relative and absolute truths for his heart-sons, Rechung Dorje Drakpa, Shiwa Ö, Sebenrepa, and Ngantson Dunpa, as well as for others. During a break in the teachings, the elders among the *repas* approached Milarepa, saying, "*Jetsun*, we are concerned that you are now getting quite old. One of these days, you may go to the *Pure Land*. If that happens, we will need someone to act in your stead, to guide us through our problems and questions, and to help us progress along the path. Our benefactors will also need a lama to help them accumulate merit.

"Who do you think could take over for you? Whoever it is, he should be given the complete *pith-instructions* of your lineage, like pouring *nectar* from one vase into another, and should be properly recognized and empowered as a lineage holder. Without such a successor, we are afraid that our precious teachings and lineage will not spread very far, and our disciples will not receive the proper guidance."

Jetsun Milarepa listened attentively to their request. At first he seemed to be slightly displeased, but then he replied, "Yes, I certainly shall have a good disciple, one who will fully receive my teachings, and develop them greatly. This evening I will see where he is. Come back early tomorrow morning and I will let you know what I see."

Milarepa arose earlier than usual the next morning and summoned all his disciples and patrons. He said to them, "The proper Dharma vessel, the man who will receive and uphold my ear-whispered teachings like the pouring from one vessel into another, will come soon. He is a fully ordained monk who also has the title 'Physician.' He will uphold my doctrine and will spread it throughout the ten directions.

"Last night I dreamed that he arrived with an empty crystal vase, and I filled his crystal vase with nectar from my silver vase.

"This old father now has a son, a son who will do good for countless living beings! He will shed light on the teachings of the Buddha just as the rising sun illuminates the earth. What more could a father want? Oh, I am so joyful and happy!"

And in that jubilant spirit, Milarepa sang this song:

> I prostrate to all the lamas,
> I pray to all the gracious ones.

In the east, the snow lion's milk is found,
It may be very wholesome and full of highest power,
Yet unless one tastes it, one will
Never know its great potential.
Only if one tastes it
Can its great flavor be felt most deeply.
Yet only the deva Indra can imbibe it.

In the south, the lordly tiger
Pounces with all his might.
Magnificent though this is,
One will never understand it,
Without an actual fight.
Only vying with a tiger
Lets one really know its pounce.
Still, only Heruka *Dombhi* rides the tiger.

In the west, the undulating turmo fish has a bitter tasting gall.
Nothing in the world could taste as bitter.
Yet without directly sampling it,
No one could imagine what it's like.
Only after tasting it
Can one fully know its bitterness.
But only naga kings and Gawojokpo can eat it.

In the north, the mighty turquoise dragon has great strength.
Yet without an actual battle,
One never feels its might.
Only wrestling with the dragon
Reveals fully its true power.
But only warrior deva *Ge Lugha* can match it.

The eastern snow lioness' milk
Must be served with a golden ladle,
Not with any common ladle,
Or the ladle will break and the milk will spill.
The essential teaching of Lords Naropa and Maitripa
Is very deep and most profound,
Yet if one does not practice it,
One never sees the depth within.
Only after practicing it
Can one understand its profundity.
This is my father Marpa's teaching.
This is what Milarepa practiced.

Milarepa's experience, insight, and instructions
Are always very effective and precise.
Yet those of little substance cannot receive them,
They are only given to the capable student.
Yet they all will be transmitted
To the monk, my coming heir.

And so Milarepa sang this song.

5 The Three Beggars

One spring day, Venerable Gampopa went for a walk outside the grounds of his house. The sky was clear and blue, the sun was shining brightly, and after many days spent indoors meditating and studying the scriptures, he was glad to get a chance to invigorate his body in the crisp mountain air. He set out to circumambulate a holy stupa.

Not far away from the monastery gate he chanced upon three beggars sitting around a fire. A famine had afflicted the region that year, and these three beggars were very hungry. As he had to pass nearby, Gampopa overheard the conversation of this ragged trio as they discussed their sorry lot.

The first was saying, "During times like this, the kind monks of Gyachakri usually give Dharma teachings that are open to all Buddhists."

He grinned and added in a sly tone, "Afterwards they also invite everyone to share a meal with them! Once we have finished eating, we can also beg some of the leftover porridge, and then find a pleasant spot nearby and feast some more! How about that?"

The second beggar replied, "I have a better idea. I wish that a cup of *tsampa* would just fall right down from the sky, with lots of butter, too. Then we could mix it with tea, add a little pepper, eh? Then off to that abandoned house to the east of the monastery, where we could all eat until we're good and full!"

The third beggar, who was the eldest of the trio, tossed some fresh sticks onto the fire. The coals crackled and the flames that rose illuminated the faces of the three. Then the old beggar spoke. "Ssshh! Look over there. A lama is coming. If he hears us, it'll wreck your plan to get fed at Gyachakri. We'd be humiliated!

"Mark my words, a good bird always soars like a vulture, even if it's starving, and a clever man always laughs and smiles, even if he's famished. Make sure not to let on how hungry you are!

"Anyway, why just wish for food? If you're going to dream, may as well dream big! Why not wish to become a king, like Tsede of Tibet, with all his wealth and power, protecting and spreading the Dharma all over the country?

"Or wish to become a great yogi, like Milarepa, eh? He's the king of yogis, that one is. He's a real ascetic, living in those snow covered mountains to the west, keeping alive on the food of meditation, wearing only a thin cotton robe. He doesn't need to sit around a fire like we do, that's for sure. He keeps his body warm with the inner heat of the blissful *tummo* yoga. They say he doesn't need to beg for food. They say the *dakinis* themselves come and feed him nectar! Now there's a yogi who practices Mahamudra day and night. And when he travels from one place to another, he flies!

"Yes, if you're going to make wishes, wish to be a yogi like Milarepa. I'll tell you, that's the best wish you could make, to renounce the world and practice Dharma as Milarepa does. Ah, but if that's too much, then you should wish to have the blessing to see his face at least once in this sorry lifetime!" And upon saying these words, the old beggar began to weep.

When Gampopa heard the name of Milarepa, the great faith that spontaneously arose in him was so powerful that he fainted, as if stricken, and remained unconscious for half a day. When he finally revived, his heart became completely enraptured and tears of devotion burst forth from his eyes. He felt like a passionate youth seeing a beautiful woman for the first time. He felt exhilarated; his whole body tingled, almost quivered, like the sudden rustling of the leaves of an aspen tree stirred by the wind.

The monk Sonam Rinchen then repeatedly threw himself to the ground and prostrated toward the snow covered mountains in the west, the mountains where Milarepa lived in retreat. As he prostrated, he prayed fervently, over and over, "Oh, Jetsun, Jetsun, please have mercy on me. Please take care of me!"

Arising, he scarcely knew where he was, or what to do next. He returned to his house and went straight to his meditation room. He sat down, lit a candle and incense, and tried to do his main practice, the *Seven Branch Prayer*. He began to sing the words of the *sadhana* as he had hundreds of times before, but since he was still in an altered state, he was unable to concentrate. He couldn't seem to make any sense out of the practice, and wondered, "What is happening to my mind?" All he could think of was Milarepa, Milarepa. All he wanted to do was to go and learn from Milarepa.

Later that night, before going to sleep, Sonam Rinchen sat down to meditate once again. Like the calm after a storm, his mind, which had been so exceedingly agitated and excited earlier in the day, now became extraordinarily calm and clear. As the night grew deeper and quieter, so too did his concentration grow brighter and stronger. Soon Gampopa achieved the state of perfect one-pointedness of mind, and saw that all outer phenomena were empty. The thought arose, "Perhaps I can now see into the minds of sentient beings as described in the sutras and tantras." As soon as he thought this, he experienced the *siddhi* of supernatural knowledge, and was thus able to read the minds of all sentient beings. As he rested in meditative equipoise, the night passed quickly, and soon the first rays of dawn were flooding Sonam Rinchen's shrine room.

With a sense of purpose and confidence unlike anything he had ever felt before, Sonam Rinchen arose from his seat, washed, put on fresh garb, and went out in search of the beggars.

A few inquiries led him to a nearby inn, where he found the beggars still asleep. He waited patiently until they awoke. Surprised to find that a highborn monk had come to visit them, the three quickly rose to their feet and placed their palms together in greeting. Their surprise was even greater when Sonam Rinchen replied, "Auspicious blessings to you. Welcome to Gyachakri. You must be hungry from your long travels. I would be honored to have you join me for breakfast."

Unable to believe their good fortune, all three beggars pondered for a moment whether this was really happening, whether they were still asleep and dreaming, or whether they had died of hunger during the night and gone to the Pure Land of Buddha Amitabha. They looked closely at the young monk, hesitating. Their spell was finally broken when the elder beggar's stomach growled loudly, and they eagerly accepted Sonam Rinchen's invitation.

Soon they were sitting around the physician monk's table in his spacious quarters, where he served them meat, tsampa and tea, in quantity and quality far exceeding anything they could have imagined. Never in their lives had they eaten so well. Afterwards they all sat back in their chairs, completely full, happy, and satisfied.

Sonam Rinchen then said to them, "Yesterday, I was out for a walk, and I happened to pass by where you were warming yourselves around the fire. I could not help overhearing you mention an inspiring yogi lama who has great renunciation and siddhis. Can you tell me where he is, who his teacher was, what teachings he gives, and what other qualities he has?"

The two younger beggars replied, "We know very little about this lama."

But then the elder beggar spoke. "Ah, yes, that one. He is called Milarepa. He stays at Gungthang, west of Lhasa, and his master was Marpa the Translator, the disciple of the great Indian pandit, Naropa. Milarepa teaches the Six Yogas of Naropa from the Hevajra Tantra. Though many people come to visit him, sometimes they cannot find him. Some see him as a white stupa, others perceive him as the Buddha Shakyamuni, so it seems like he can appear in many different forms. I, myself, have never seen him."

Gampopa then said, "Still, it seems that you know a great deal about him. I would be most grateful if you would guide me to his place. I have sixteen ounces of gold, and will give you half, so that you too may study the Dharma if you wish. The other half I must keep to provide for myself."

The old man replied, with tears in his eyes, "Certainly! I will gladly guide you to him."

That night, Gampopa made offerings and heartfully invoked the *Three Jewels*. He went to sleep praying one-pointedly to Milarepa. In his dreams, he saw himself blowing a fantastically long brass trumpet, whose mighty sound pervaded every corner of the earth. People were commenting that there was no larger trumpet in all of Ü. He then beat a tremendous gong.

A young lady appeared in his dream, dressed in the fashion of Mon. She handed him a massive drum, saying, "Beat it so that all humankind may hear." Gampopa hung the drum in the sky and beat a rhythm upon it, sending out a solemn, pleasant, and penetrating sound across the face of the earth. Many wild animals heard the drumbeat and many people gathered around. The lady then said to him, "You beat the drum for human beings, but many animals have also been blessed by the sound."

She then handed him a skull-cup full of milk, saying, "Please offer this milk to all beings of the animal world. Drink of it yourself when you thirst. Gampopa replied, "Surely this milk is not enough for so many animals." The lady responded, "When you drink this milk, you will benefit not only these animals but all sentient beings of the six realms. Now I am going to the west." Then she disappeared.

Much later in his life Gampopa commented, "The human beings who heard my drum that night are those students of lesser capacity who must go through the stages of the path in a gradual manner. The treasure of the Gradual Path to Enlightenment given to us by the Kadampa lamas is truly great. The animals who heard my drum are my great yogi disciples who practice meditation in caves. This dream also revealed that I would go to my guru, Milarepa, and rely solely on his instructions in the skillful path and Mahamudra."

When he awoke in the morning, he decided to go to Milarepa at once. He sold his house and land, collected sixteen ounces of gold and some tea, and went to say goodbye to his Kadampa teachers. They were all greatly disappointed to hear that he was leaving them. His teacher, Geshe Chennawa said, "We shaped the copper gong, but another shall make it resound. We ordained you and prepared you as a student of Buddhadharma, but it shall be another guru who will lead you to fruition. We are very sad that you are leaving us. You have kept your monastic vows purely, and no teacher could have asked for a better student.

"Still, we can see that your departure is inevitable. Your karmic connection to the yogi Milarepa is clearly evident, so go with our blessings, Bhikshu Sonam Rinchen. But whatever you may do, remember us. Do not give up our monastic traditions."[3]

Thus receiving permission, Gampopa, accompanied by the old beggar, set out to find Milarepa.

6 In Search of Milarepa

In the course of their journey, Sonam Rinchen sometimes murmured, sometimes spoke, and sometimes cried aloud, "Oh, when can I see my guru?"

His longing to see Milarepa was so great that tears never left his eyes, and the thought of stopping for rest or comfort never entered his mind. He slept neither at night nor by day; he simply walked on and on to meet Milarepa.

This made the journey very hard on the old beggar, who, although pious and true, was not ablaze with the one-pointed zeal that charged Gampopa's tireless pace. The beggar's feet blistered, his muscles burned, his old bones ached as they never had before in his hard life. He yearned for nothing more than a warm fire, a hot cup of yak butter tea, and a sheltered place to lie down and rest his weary old body. But he was of tough stock, and dared not speak up. So on they drove, with Gampopa leading the way like a man possessed.

Finally, when they arrived at Tsang in Upper Nyang, the old beggar's body gave out and he fell sick. He said to Gampopa, "Master, I'm sorry. I am really sick. I can't go any further. Please don't offer to wait for me. I wouldn't think to slow you down. Anyway, I don't know much about the way from here on. I do know that there's a monastery just down the road called Sajya. I can rest there, and you can ask them for directions. They should be able to tell you how to go from here."

Gampopa let the old beggar lean on him for support, and it was not long before they reached the monastery. Gampopa made a very generous offering to the monks and asked them to provide medical care, lodging, and food for the poor old man, which they readily agreed to do. Handing the old man a sack of gold, Gampopa thanked him for telling him of Milarepa and for helping him thus far, and bid him goodbye. The monks gave him the directions he needed, and he set out alone to find Milarepa.

Gampopa walked and walked, yet the land scarcely seemed to change. At a fork in the road he made a wrong turn onto a trail that led nowhere, and he lost several hours finding his way back. The path divided unexpectedly several more times, and each time he was uncertain whether he had taken the right fork or not. No other travelers happened along, and he began to fear that he was lost.

He had felt confident with the old beggar guiding him, but now he felt like a blind man wandering through unfamiliar territory. He did not know whether to push on or go back, and the sun was already hidden behind a towering mountain range.

Soon night fell on this barren land, a new moon night that rapidly engulfed the physician monk in pitch blackness. When he started on his journey Gampopa's energy had been so roused with devoted ardor that he could have walked across all Tibet without stopping. Now, wrapped in utter darkness, unable to advance or retreat, a wave of intense frustration and despair swept over him, and he curled up on the ground, covered his face with his hands and wept bitterly as he prayed to Jetsun Milarepa.

After some time, he thought he heard a voice through his sobbing. He opened his eyes and saw someone standing over him, holding a lantern. He sat up, and to his complete astonishment, he found himself staring into the old beggar's kindly face!

"Here! Don't cry like that!" he said. "I'll guide you to your guru. After I had a little rest and some hot food and tea, I felt my old self again. I don't know what was in that tea, but the truth be told, I've never felt so full of vigor and strength in all my life. Whatever it was, this is wild country, as you rightly know, and I got to worrying about you. So I hopped out of bed, bought this lamp from the monks, and set out to catch up with you."

Gampopa was so overjoyed to see the old man that he was laughing and crying at the same time, and the old man seemed just as relieved to have found Gampopa. The elder had gathered some dry dung along the road, and before long a crackling fire brought cheer to the dark night. Then they slept, but Gampopa was up before dawn, and they were on their way again long before the first rays of sunlight broke over the mountains.

Soon the road joined with another road and widened. They could see it stretching for many miles across the wide valley. Pleased that the way seemed clear once again, Gampopa turned to express his relief to his companion, and then stared in amazement at the empty road behind him. The old man had simply vanished! Only moments before, he had heard the beggar's labored breathing. Now it was as if the old man had never been there at all.

Stunned, Gampopa sat down. Then he thought of Jetsun Milarepa again, and immediately great peace filled his being. Like a haze lifting, he realized that the old beggar, indeed all three beggars, had been emanations of his guru, Milarepa. All along the guru had been aware of him, drawing him, guiding and protecting him. Gampopa rose and made many prostrations in the direction of the guru's retreat.

Gampopa then continued on his journey, feeling renewed. The road he was on was well traveled, and he was able to ask directions along the way. When he reached Dronso Charwa he met some tradesmen coming down from the highlands, and asked them if they knew of Milarepa.

One of the merchants, a man called Dawa Zungpo of Nyanang, replied, "Ah, Milarepa! He is great, a master of *yoga*. He is really an accomplished guru. He is known all over Tibet, everyone has heard of him. He is now staying at Chuwar in Drin."

When he heard this, Gampopa became so excited that he thought the merchant was Milarepa himself. He rushed to hug the startled merchant, and then burst into tears.

Now with great confidence, Gampopa set off toward Chuwar in Drin. After walking many miles, he came to the center of a great plain. It was there that his grueling pace finally caught up with him. Exhausted, he sat down to rest on a rock. He was overcome by hunger and fatigue, and his entire energy system had become unbalanced and disordered. He fainted, and fell from the rock to the ground. There he lay unconscious for half a day.

When at last he came to, every inch of his body from head to toe was throbbing with pain. He was parched with thirst, but so great was his pain that he was unable to move. No one passed by to help him as he lay in agonizing pain, without food or water, for two long days and two long nights.

On the third day, feeling as if death might be near, Gampopa spoke these words with utter conviction, through parched cracked lips and with tears streaming down his dusty face:

"If I cannot see the Jetsun in this life, then in the three *bardos* after my death I will look only to him as my sole refuge. I swear I will be born near him in the next life, and that my mind will then be united with his."

Then he lay back and wept, awaiting his fate.

Before long, a Kadampa monk from Cha Yul came walking along the road. Seeing Gampopa lying by the side of the road, the monk approached him and said, "Auspicious blessings. Where are you going?"

Gampopa was so weak and his mouth and throat were so dry that he could barely speak. He strained to reply, and said in a rasping whisper, "Nowhere at the moment."

"What is your destination?"

"I am going to Drin, to visit Jetsun Milarepa."

"Ah. I am also going in that direction. Are you sick?"

"Yes, indeed, and I am also very thirsty," said Gampopa. "Could you give me a drink of water?"

"Of course, my brother," the monk replied, and produced a bowl from his purse, which he filled from his water bag and offered to Gampopa.

After drinking it, Gampopa felt much relieved. His pain abated and his strength began to return. The monk offered him some food as well, and soon Gampopa felt completely refreshed and invigorated. Then, in the company of the kind monk, he set off again on his journey.

Meanwhile, Jetsun Milarepa, in a very happy spirit, was teaching the Dharma at Joyful Fortune Peak. In the midst of the discourse, he would sometimes stop and remain silent for a while, and then suddenly laugh heartily.

One of his disciples, a gifted lady patron from Drin, known as Tsese, asked him, "Dear Jetsun, what is it? Why are you suddenly remaining silent and then suddenly bursting into laughter? Are you laughing because you are happy with the progress of some gifted disciple, and silent when you see the confusion and wrong thoughts of one of your slow students?"

"Neither," replied Milarepa.

"Then why did you smile and laugh today?" asked Tsese.

"Because now, my son, the monk from Ü, has arrived at Dingri. There he fainted and fell and lay in great pain beside a rock. In his agony he cried out to me for help, in tears and with great faith and sincerity. I felt pity for him, and in my samadhi I sent him blessings, whereupon help quickly came to him. Seeing that, I felt very moved and joyful, and laughed out loud."

As he told this story, tears welled up in Milarepa's eyes.

"When will he arrive here?"

"Sometime between tomorrow and the day after."

"Will we have the good karma of seeing this man?"

"Oh, yes! And whoever has the privilege of preparing his seat when he arrives will be nourished by the *food of samadhi*. Whoever has the blessing of first seeing him will be guided to the blissful pure land of liberation!"

7 Arrival

The next day Gampopa and the Kadampa monk arrived at a village
near Trashigang. There they saw a woman weaving. Gampopa approached and asked the woman, "Do you know where Jetsun Milarepa
lives, a great yogi who can read other people's minds and perform
other miracles?"

"I will take you to a woman who knows about this," she replied.

She led Gampopa to an elderly lady dressed in white cotton clothes.
The lady had a big stomach, with a bulky sash wrapped around it.
Gampopa politely asked her of Milarepa's whereabouts.

The elderly lady asked him, "From where do you come, sir?"

Gampopa replied, "My name is Sonam Rinchen. I have come from
the sunlit province of Ü, to visit Jetsun Milarepa."

"Ah, yes," said the woman. "Well, in that case, I will help you, but
you cannot reach where he stays tonight. You are welcome to stay the
night in the upstairs of my house, you can follow me there now. I
would be honored to offer you some food."

The elderly lady had a fine house, newly painted and very clean
and fresh. Inside, she happily served them tea, cakes, and other re-
freshments.

When they were well satisfied, the elderly woman said, "Jetsun
Milarepa knew that you were coming. Yesterday morning I went to
see him, and while I was in his presence he said, 'A Kadampa monk
from U is coming to see me. Whoever brings him to meet me will no
longer need to fear rebirth in the lower realms.' He also made a prophecy about your future. With his omniscient eyes he knew of your sickness and fatigue at Dingri, and he blessed you in his samadhi.

"I received permission from him to be the first to welcome you. My daughter is also a meditator, and a devoted student of the Jetsun. He has told her that a noble son of a noble family will come to be his student, and that we must assist him in every way. My daughter will come tomorrow and take you to him. So, please stay with us this evening."

Hearing this, Gampopa thought to himself, "It truly was the grace of the guru that saved my life at Dingri. He knew of my coming all along. Judging from his praise and predictions, I must be a worthy vessel indeed!"

Thinking thus, Gampopa became a little proud of himself. As his self-conceit grew, he felt certain that he would have no difficulty now in receiving oral instructions.

The next morning the daughter arrived and took Gampopa to meet Milarepa. Sonam Rinchen's excitement and pride seemed to grow greater and greater with every step as they approached Milarepa's camp. The moment he had longed for was here at last. Or at least so he thought.

But as they entered the yogi's camp they were greeted instead by Sebenrepa, one of Milarepa's close disciples. Sebenrepa was carrying a bundle of firewood, a bag of tea, and a cooking pot. He greeted them and said to Gampopa, "Monk from U, I am called Sebenrepa. Jetsun Milarepa has sent me with a message for you. He says to tell you that you have become full of yourself. You have developed pride. He will not grant you an audience today. Please come with me."

Sebenrepa led a stunned Gampopa to a rocky cave nearby. He handed Gampopa the firewood, tea and cooking pot, and told him, "The Jetsun wishes that you stay here alone until you have purified the stain of pride. He will not see you for at least half a moon. Keep this wood and tea. I will supply you with provisions."

Sebenrepa then added, "The guru knew that you were coming, monk from U, and he intends to give you the oral instructions. So don't be disheartened. Stay here and supplicate him."

Thus, Gampopa had to stay under the rocky roof of a cave for half a month, waiting, to purify his prideful attitude. After a half month's time he had lost all hope and all fear. He expected nothing. It was then that the elderly woman's daughter came again to his cave and said, "Jetsun Milarepa wishes to see you. Come, you will meet him now at Joyful Fortune Hill!"

8 Meeting the Guru

Gampopa followed the young woman to the top of Joyful Fortune Hill. There, at the summit, Gampopa saw his guru, Jetsun Milarepa, for the first time.

Milarepa was sitting on top of a huge boulder. He looked to be about eighty years old. His long dark hair, mixed with white, fell loosely over his shoulders and down below his waist. He wore only a thin robe of white cotton, scarcely enough to keep a man warm in the brisk mountain air of Tibet. His skin was weathered from years of living outdoors, yet he seemed to radiate an aura of abundant energy and peace. His eyes shone with the inner light born from years of meditation. Gampopa felt as if he had come into the presence of a lion or a king.

Full of reverence and sincerity, Gampopa prostrated before the guru, and offered him all sixteen ounces of gold as a *mandala* offering, along with a brick of fine tea. Milarepa looked straight ahead for a while without responding. Then, with his eyes still fixed, he picked up a piece of gold from the mandala, tossed it into the sky, and said, "I offer this to Marpa of Lodrak."

When he said this, celestial music filled the air and a heavenly light shone all around them, creating an indescribably magnificent atmosphere. Milarepa picked up a human skull-cup filled with nectar, drank half of it, and handed the remainder to Gampopa, saying, "Drink it up."

At this point, Gampopa noticed that he was not alone with Milarepa. In fact, they were surrounded by many of Milarepa's students, who were yogis. Now, Gampopa had taken full ordination as a Kadampa

monk, and was supposed to abstain from alcohol. He thought to himself, "I am a monk, and there are many students watching. I cannot drink this." Thinking thus, he hesitated.

"Don't think so much. Just drink it," said Milarepa.

Strong faith welled up in Gampopa's heart, washing away all doubts. "The guru knows," Gampopa thought, and drained the skull-cup, leaving not one drop. This confirmed to Milarepa that Gampopa was indeed a worthy vessel for his ear-whispered teachings, and that Gampopa would receive all of Milarepa's transmission without exception. It also meant that Gampopa would fully realize these teachings through practice, and become a lineage holder.

"What is your name?" asked Milarepa.

"I am called Sonam Rinchen," Gampopa replied.

Milarepa closed his eyes and said, "Sonam Rinchen, Sonam Rinchen, Sonam Rinchen. You are here because you've gathered immeasurable merit (Sonam). You are truly very precious (Rinchen) to all sentient beings."

Thus Milarepa repeated three times the meaning of Gampopa's name, and thought to himself, "Whoever so much as hears the name of this son of mine will be liberated from samsara. But I had best not speak of it now."

Gampopa then related the story of his journey from U, and with great anticipation and earnestness asked the Jetsun to tell his life story.

Looking deeply into Gampopa's eyes, Milarepa replied solemnly, "Our connection is very profound and deep. Although you have just arrived here, we have never been separate, my son."[4]

A shiver of joy coursed through Gampopa. He remembered when the old beggar had vanished on his journey, and how he had felt great peace when he realized that all three beggars were Milarepa's emanations. The Jetsun's words and the look in his eyes confirmed Gampopa's prior intuitions beyond any doubt.

After a while, Milarepa said to Gampopa, "It is very wonderful that you have great faith in me, and have come here from so far away to see me." Then he recited a verse,

> Gold and this old man do not agree,
> And I have no pot in which to boil the tea.

And he gave back the gold and tea, saying, "Here, you keep this gold, keep this tea as well. You may need them yourself, as provisions for your practice. As for my life story, I will sing you a song. Shiwa Ö!

Rechungpa! Both of you come here. We should sing a song of welcome to this monk!"
Then, accompanied by his two disciples, Mila sang,

> In the sky of *dharmakaya*,
> Beyond the reach of idle chatter,
> Where clouds of ever-flowing compassion gather,
> I bow at the feet of gracious Marpa,
> The protector and refuge of all beings.

> On my right sits son Rechungpa,
> On my left sits Shiwa Ö.
> Both join me in chorus to sing
> A song of welcome for you, Physician!

> In the holy land of India,
> Though many teachers boasted much,
> The two most famous gurus were
> The great Naropa and Maitripa,
> Who, sun and moon-like, lit the world.
> Marpa Lotsawa was their heart-son.
> He mastered all the Buddha's teachings,
> Was the host of all mandalas,
> Attracted capable disciples.
> Hearing of this learned Master,
> Praised by all of the dakinis,
> From my depths, I yearned to see him.

> I searched for him with all my strength.
> On meeting him, I swooned in bliss.
> Bowing at his lotus feet,
> I sought the most profound transmission
> That would, in this very lifetime,
> Lead me to full Buddhahood.

> My father, Buddha, said to me then,
> 'By the mercy of Naropa
> I possess this knife-like teaching,
> Sharp enough to cut the cords
> That bind one to endless samsara.'

> Exerting body, speech and mind,
> A pauper, I worked hard to please him.
> Seeing my fervor and devotion
> With omniscient eyes, he told me,
> 'The Teachings of the *four transmissions*
> Are no longer perfect now,
> Some are lacking, some excessive.

Even though one risks a headache
Imparting them to one's disciples,
Little profit can this bring.
In days of defilement such as these ones,
Folks have little time for leisure.
Instead their lives are always filled
With constant vain activities.
Son, don't waste your time in studies,
But *practice* the essential teachings.'

To repay my guru's bounty,
And end for good the fear of death,
I meditated with conviction,
And transformed negative patterns into blessings.
Seeing the essence of the *three poisons*,
I realized the spontaneously perfect *trikaya*.
To my capable disciples
I'll transmit the inner experience.
This, along with all the blessings,
To you, Physician, I will pass
The most profound oral instructions.
As you put these into practice,
You will spread the Buddhadharma.
Bear this in mind, dear Physician,
And soon you'll relax, in the state free from craving.
This is my life story in brief.
Details can wait until some other time.

My son, if you want to practice
The sacred Dharma wholeheartedly,
Don't seek only this life's pleasure.
Think instead of your next life.
If you'd be a lineage holder
Of the whispered Kagyu doctrine,
Don't just enjoy words, find their meaning.
You, O monk, remember this.

Sir, you asked for my life story.
In answer, I have sung this song.

Milarepa then said, with joy in his eyes, "This is my welcome to
our dear physician bhikshu."

Gampopa could not remember another time in his life when he
had been so happy, so peaceful, so completely fulfilled. He felt as if
he had just returned home after a long journey.

He wanted to give Milarepa an offering to express his love, devotion and gratitude for his guru's kindness. He saw that one of the repas had built a small fire nearby for cooking. Gampopa excused himself, and taking the tea that Milarepa had returned to him, went back to his cave to fetch a small kettle that Sebenrepa had given him. He took the kettle down to the sunny banks of the mountain stream nearby. There was a little waterfall, and there Gampopa reached into the cold water and filled the kettle.

The repa who had built the cook fire was happy to let Gampopa set his kettle in the red hot coals. Soon the pure mountain water was briskly boiling. Gampopa brewed up a delicious pot of tea, and carried it to where Milarepa was sitting with Shiwa Ö and Rechungpa. Setting the tea down before the Jetsun, he said, smiling, "Precious Lama, please accept this offering, a small token of my gratitude and veneration for you."

Milarepa accepted it gladly. He invited Gampopa, Shiwa Ö and Rechungpa to join him, and they all enjoyed their hot tea together in quiet mindfulness, appreciating its delicate flavor, and the soothing feeling of the cup warming their hands in the crisp mountain air.

After they had emptied the tea kettle, Gampopa started to rise so that he could brew up a fresh pot, but Milarepa gently stopped him, saying to Rechungpa, "Now we should offer this monk some tea in return. Please go and ask each repa here for a bit of tea."

So Rechungpa went and collected some tea from every repa in the camp, and having done so, he brewed another pot. He brought it back to Milarepa, who gave the tea a special blessing,[5] making it extraordinarily delicious.

Thus did Jetsun Milarepa, together with his yogi disciples, happily welcome the monk Gampopa into their camp.

9 Initiations and Instructions

The next morning Milarepa wished to travel to Chuwar in Manlung. Eager to remain in Milarepa's presence, Gampopa asked if he might accompany him on his journey, and the guru gladly assented. After a hearty breakfast of hot tsampa and yak butter tea, they were on their way.

When they arrived in Chuwar, they went to a large cave where Milarepa had often meditated. There Gampopa asked the Jetsun to bless him, and for the purpose of establishing a spiritual relationship, to give him some instruction.

"What empowerments and teachings have you received before?" Milarepa asked.

Gampopa replied that he had received the four empowerments of Guhyasamaja, the Hevajra empowerment, the magnificent blessings of Dakmema, the teachings of *Luipa*, the magnificent blessings of the Six-Ornament *Vajravarahi* from Lama Lodru of Maryul, and many empowerments from other lamas. He also told Milarepa that he had been able to remain seated in meditation for seven days.

Milarepa just laughed and said, "So what? You sit for seven days and don't experience the *clear light*. You can't get oil from pressing sand, you get it by pressing mustard seeds. Practice my *Short AH Tummo Yoga*, if you really want to see the true nature of mind. The Tibetans did not allow Atisha to teach the *tantras*."

Gampopa said, "But there are many tantric teachings in Kadampa."

Milarepa replied, "Yes, there are tantric teachings, but no quintessential instructions there.[6] Although there is a complete generation and completion process in a single meditation practice, this is merely the samadhi of analysis.[7] Meditating on the selflessness of the stages of the path has only a relative value. Practice meditation on the *Method Path*.[8]

"I do not mean that your previous initiations are not good, those are excellent and profound teachings that you received. I just want to stress the importance of a correct karmic relationship with the guru, and the absolute necessity for you to receive the blessing of my lineage."[9]

Milarepa then blessed Gampopa and initiated him into the Sindura Vajrayogini practice of the Whispered Lineage, and in the mandala of the deity painted in cinnabar, Gampopa received the pith-instructions. He also received the full transmission of the tummo practice. Then Gampopa went off to his cave to meditate.

After a short time of practicing in accordance with Milarepa's instructions, Gampopa began to have some profound and positive meditative experiences. Then he started to compare Milarepa's teachings with those that he had received from his other gurus. There were places where they seemed to be contradictory, and as a result, much confusion and doubt arose in his mind and he found it difficult to continue meditating.

"I am getting nowhere," Gampopa said to himself. "I must go to see the guru and cut the roots of this confusion."

That very afternoon he left his cave and sought out Milarepa. He found him by the stream, washing his bowl and sipping the fresh cold mountain water.

"How is your practice going?"

"At first it was going very well, but then many questions arose. In the *Guhyasamaja Tantra*, the *Chatuhpitha*, and other works, it says, 'There is greater merit in making offering to one hair of the guru than in making offerings of a mountain heap of jewels to all the Buddhas of the past, present, and future.' Is there a way of accumulating merit that is superior to this?"

"There is," Milarepa replied.

"Please teach me about this."

"If you practice the oral teachings that the guru has given, without wasting them, that is it," said Milarepa.

Gampopa was silent for a while, drinking in the meaning of the guru's answer. Then he spoke again.

"I asked Geshe Nyugrumpa if it is possible to attain Buddhahood in one life, in one body. His reply was, 'Yes, but to do that, one must not have a hair's consideration for this life.' I then asked the same question to Geshe Yarlungpa, and he said, 'That is not the true meaning. That is just the figurative meaning. You can attain Buddhahood: by taking a medicine pill, which will make you immortal like the sun and moon; or, in the seventh lifetime of practice; or, by actually seeing the divine *yidam*; or, if you are able to travel to the celestial realms.' Which of these answers is true?"

Milarepa replied, "The words of Geshe Nyugrumpa are not only the figurative meaning, they are also the true meaning. You must have no consideration for this life.

"If an authentic guru has disciples who are worthy vessels, who receive the complete empowerment in the Mantrayana mandala, and who practice both *generation stage* and *completion stage* meditation continually, in accord with the oral instructions, then those students of the highest potential will attain Buddhahood in this lifetime; those of medium potential will attain it just before they die, or in the bardo. Even if the students are extremely lazy, they will attain it in seven or sixteen lifetimes. If they cannot attain this, they must have corrupted their vows, and for a while they might be reborn in the lower realms.

"In general, physician monk, you should not trust those who philosophize. Do not listen to them. Do not follow them. Trust instead those who practice meditation. Listen to them, follow them.

"The best recommendation is to hold to holy ones who have let go of the concerns of this life. Anyone who is led along by this life will only teach you the eight worldly dharmas.

"You should also know that there are four ways of misunderstanding emptiness: losing emptiness in labelling; losing emptiness in the basic nature of all knowables; losing emptiness in the antidote; and losing emptiness by attachment to emptiness.

"Losing emptiness in labelling means merely saying, 'All objects of the ordinary rational mind of dualistic grasping are non-existent.'[10] If you say that, this is losing emptiness in labelling.

"Losing emptiness in the basic nature of all knowables is merely conceptually saying, 'All phenomena, or samsara and nirvana, are empty.' If you say that, this is losing emptiness in the basic nature of all knowables.

"Losing emptiness in the antidote is saying, 'Afflictive emotions and discursive thoughts—whatever arises—if you look right at it, that is emptiness.' This is holding the dualistic notion that negative thoughts and conflicting emotions are something to be abandoned and that emptiness is the antidote.[11]

"Losing emptiness by attachment to emptiness is saying, 'There is nothing to meditate on whatsoever, so all meditation is emptiness.' It is also thinking that emptiness is a goal to be realized, that the ground, the path, and the fruit are separate, and that by following the path one will obtain the goal of realizing emptiness.[12]

"These are not the perfect path. However, for a beginner there is a small benefit in initially using these kinds of thoughts to reverse clinging to intrinsic reality.

"In general, if you do not fully realize the true nature of your mind in the deepest sense, even if you temporarily experience bliss, *luminosity* and non-thought, you will not transcend the three worlds. These are known as temporary experiences because they do not resolve the mind to its depths. If you ask, 'What is the true path?' It is when an authentic guru gives the student who is a worthy vessel initiation and instruction.

"Primordial awareness exists pervasively in all sentient beings. All the Buddhas are luminosity in the dharmakaya. Yogis practice meditation using an infinite variety of skillful methods, and thus they can naturally realize the view. Conflicting emotions naturally cease. Dualistic thoughts are effortlessly self-liberated, and wisdom spontaneously dawns. At this time, one's realization and experience cannot be expressed in words. It is like the ecstasy of a young woman, or the dream of a deaf mute. Although this ground is in all sentient beings, they fail to recognize it. Therefore, it is very important to follow a guru who holds a lineage.

"Primordial awareness has no origins. Its gateway cannot be blocked in any way. It cannot be shown by any analogy. It cannot be described by any words. It cannot be demonstrated by any sophistry. Therefore, we should not try to fabricate it. Just let go and relax in the realm of the natural state of mind."

Milarepa then sang this song:

> Looking at your own mind is the view, O, physician monk.
> This certainly is the highest view.
> If you look for the view outside of your mind,
> It's like a blind rich person leaving home in search of gold.
>
> Don't clear away the "faults" of dullness and mental agitation, O,
>   physician monk.
> This is certainly the highest meditation.
> If you try to drive these "faults" away,
> It's like lighting a butter lamp in broad daylight.

Stop alternating between acceptance and rejection,
   O, physician monk.
This is certainly the highest action.
If you are always accepting and rejecting,
It's like a bee trapped in a spider's web.

Rest at ease with confidence in the view, O, physician monk.
That is certainly the highest *samaya*.
If you search for the samaya elsewhere, without observing this
   precept,
It's like trying to reverse the flow of a river.

Develop deep awareness in your mind, O, physician monk.
This is certainly the highest fruition itself.
If you search elsewhere for the fruition of spontaneous
   self-perfection,
It's like a frog trying to leap into the sky.

Find the guru within your own mind, O, physician monk.
That is certainly the highest guru.
If you search elsewhere for a guru,
It's like trying to abandon your own mind.
In short, O, physician monk,
Everything that appears is nothing other than mind.

When Milarepa finished his song, he looked at Gampopa and smiled
with shining eyes. As on the day of their first meeting, Gampopa again
felt the brilliant regal presence of his guru, and knew with unshakable
confidence that Jetsun Milarepa had spoken from direct experience of
the true nature of mind. All of his prior questions, doubts, and confusion vanished like morning dew in the sun-like presence of his guru.

"What the Jetsun has said is absolutely right," Gampopa thought.

He thanked Milarepa, and returning to his cave, he renewed his
meditation practice with even greater diligence, enthusiasm, and confidence than before.

10 Tummo Retreat

The first night of his retreat, Gampopa meditated naked in a cave near the juncture of two valleys. Although he was naked and the night air was cold, blissful warmth arose within him spontaneously, and in this rapturous state he passed the night. Just before dawn he fell asleep, but his body remained rock steady in an upright sitting position. For seven days he meditated in this way, and continued to experience inner warmth and great bliss, the fruits of the tummo yoga, effortlessly arising in him.

On the morning of the seventh day, he had a vision of the Buddhas of the Five Families in the five directions. The experience seemed profound, but when he reported it to Milarepa, the Jetsun replied, "This experience is like a man pressing his eyes and seeing two moons in front of him as a result. It is only due to your having captured and controlled the energy-winds[13] of the *five elements*. It is neither good nor bad. Keep meditating."

Although Milarepa had told him that this experience was of no particular significance, it inspired Gampopa. Delighted and full of enthusiasm, he continued to practice intensely for another three months.

Then one day, in the midst of his morning round of practice, just before sunrise, he suddenly experienced the feeling that all the *three thousand world systems* in the universe were spinning around like a wheel turning. He grew very dizzy, felt a wave of nausea sweep over him, and then vomited many times. Drained, he fainted and fell to the ground. He lay there, unconscious, for a long time. When he finally revived, he consulted with Milarepa, who commented, "This experience is due to the energy-winds in the *left and right channels* entering into the *central channel*. It is neither good nor bad. Just continue with your meditation."

One morning, Gampopa had a vision that his cave was thronged with *Avalokiteshvaras*. Each one had a moon disc atop his head.

He reported this to Milarepa, who said, "This is due to the increase of *bindu* in the Great Bliss *chakra* at the crown of your head. It is neither good nor bad. Keep meditating."

One evening at dusk, Gampopa saw the *Vajra Black Line Hell*. Along with this vision, his heart area became congested and felt like it was seizing up. A strong wave of *heart energy-wind* arose, stirring his entire body, and he became intensely depressed.

He asked the guru, who said, "You have tied your meditation belt too tightly. It's too short for you, and it's binding your channels, causing a constriction in your *upward moving energy-wind*. It's neither good nor bad. Loosen your belt and keep meditating."

The guru also gave Gampopa some additional inner yogic instructions for working with his *nadis, prana,* and bindu. Armed with these teachings, Gampopa returned to his cave and resumed his meditative efforts.

One day Gampopa had a particularly fascinating experience. He was able to see clearly the beings of the six realms, from the gods of the *desire realm* down to the beings in the hell realms. All of these beings were drinking and enjoying the nectar of the gods, which rained from the higher realms down into the lower realms, satisfying them all.

However, he saw his mother in a very weak position, unable to partake of the nectar. She appeared to be very thin, sickly and weak, near death from hunger and thirst.

He immediately went to see Milarepa and told him of his experience. Milarepa replied, "The rain of nectar is the increase of the bindu in your *right and left channels* in the throat center, the Chakra of Enjoyment. Your previous nausea was due to your energy-wind entering the channel system. This experience is due to the bindu coming into the channels. Your mother's inability to drink the nectar means that the mouth of your central channel has not yet opened. It is neither good nor bad. Keep on meditating, without hope or fear."

So saying, he taught Gampopa some forceful and vigorous *yantra yoga* exercises, including leaping and tumbling movements.

Gampopa returned to his meditation and practiced for another month. Then one day, due to the power of the yantra yoga movements, his body began to shiver, tremble, and shake uncontrollably; he began crying, and he felt an involuntary desire to shout. He thought, "What is happening? Am I possessed by demons?"

He went and informed his guru, who told him, "The bindu is increasing in the dharmachakra at the heart center. It is neither good nor bad. Concentrate on your yantra yoga exercises, and do not stop them."

From then on, Gampopa found that he needed little food.

One day he saw both a lunar and solar eclipse: the light of the sun and moon was completely obscured by thread-like clouds, the two thin tails of the demon *Rahu*.

Gampopa went and told his experience to Milarepa, who said, "This is caused by the energy-winds in the left and right channels entering into the central channel. It is neither good nor bad. You are a very brave man, physician monk. You are a mighty vulture indeed! Redouble your efforts."

At the end of his instructions, the guru mumbled, "There is a supreme being. Now is the time, now is the time, now is the time!" He then said nothing more.

Gampopa returned to his cave and meditated with even greater energy. After one month, a vision of the complete mandala of red Hevajra appeared before him. He thought, "The last time I saw Milarepa he said, 'Now is the time, now is the time.' He must have foreseen the appearance of this mandala of my patron yidam. This is what he meant by saying there is a supreme being. This vision must be the action of the yidam Hevajra."

He asked about the meaning of this vision, and the guru replied, "The red bindu[14] obtained from your mother, which was coming up from below, has been established and stabilized in the dharmachakra at the heart center. It is neither good nor bad. Keep meditating."

Gampopa meditated with great exertion. Then one day, he saw the mandala of the skeleton form of Chakrasamvara, as described and taught in the yogic tradition of Luipa. He asked the guru about this. Milarepa replied, "This is because your *transformation chakra* at the navel center is now filled with bindu. It is neither good nor bad. Just continue meditating."

So Gampopa meditated diligently, and after fourteen days he had the sensation that his whole body had become as vast as the sky. From head to toe, his whole body, limbs and all, was full of sentient beings of the six realms. Most of them were drinking ordinary milk, and the rest were drawing milk down from the stars, and drinking that.

He heard a roaring noise like the sound of a great storm, but he had no idea where it was coming from. At dawn he loosened his meditation belt, and the noise stopped.

He asked the guru about this, and Milarepa answered, "This was because the *karmapranas* have driven the bindu into the hundreds of thousands of channels throughout your entire body. Now is the time to transform these karmic pranas into wisdom prana." Whereupon, Milarepa imparted to Gampopa the supreme tummo instruction for realization of the state of *Vajradhara* and sent him to practice.

Gampopa continued to meditate. Then one day the whole valley of Gungthang seemed to fill with smoke. By late afternoon it was pitch black. He could not find the path, like a blind man he groped and crawled until he finally made his way to the guru's abode.

Milarepa said, "It's nothing to worry about at all. Just relax, sit here and meditate."

Milarepa then taught him the method of clearing away obstructions and blockages in the upper part of the body. Gampopa did the practice and the darkness dissipated like the dawning of day.

Then one evening Gampopa saw his whole body as a skeleton without flesh, bound together by many energy channels. He asked the Jetsun about this experience, and he replied, "You are working too hard. You are practicing your *pranayama* too forcefully. Practice more gently."

Thus, once again relying on the priceless oral instructions of his guru Milarepa to guide him along the path, Gampopa returned to his cave. His practice and experiences were now becoming very advanced. The prana flowed freely through his body now, and so he felt perfectly at ease and comfortable meditating on the bare rock surface without any meditation cushion.

In this way he continued through the rest of the day with unflagging confidence, determination, and faith.

11 Gampopa's Magnificent Dream

That evening at dusk, Gampopa meditated on his patron yidam and recited mantras. He practiced *guru yoga* at midnight, and then made many supplications and prayers to Jetsun Milarepa. Just before dawn he did a meditation practice focusing on the life-sustaining prana. Then, as dawn finally broke, he fell asleep for a short while. As he slept, he had a vivid dream in which twenty-four signs appeared, signs that bore no relationship to his normal thought patterns. When he awoke the sun was shining brightly, and he wondered, "Were these signs auspicious or were they bad omens?" He pondered this question for awhile, full of doubts and hesitation, and then it occurred to him, "Ah, I can ask my guru. He is the Buddha himself! He is omniscient! He will surely have the answer!"

With this thought in mind, he jumped up from his meditation seat and immediately went to see Milarepa, without stopping to eat breakfast, and even forgetting to put on his robe. When Gampopa arrived where Milarepa was staying he found him sleeping at the base of a rock by the Chuwar river. His clothes partially covered his face, some were bundled up beneath his head for a pillow.

Gampopa prostrated, offered a mandala, and then said excitedly, "Jetsun! Jetsun! I have something very important to tell you! Please, do not sleep! Please get up!"

"It came to me that some distracting thoughts arose in you this morning," said Milarepa as he sat up, rubbing his limbs. "Tell me, then, what is it that is so important and has you so excited today?"

Gampopa answered, "Oh, precious Guru! Some powerful omens appeared in my dreams early this morning. I do not know if they were good signs or bad. I ask you, please interpret them for me."

And Gampopa added in song,

Oh, wondrous Jetsun, cotton-clad,
Yogi who practices with incredible discipline,
Like the ornament on a crown, like a wish-fulfilling gem,
You are the renowned Mila, venerated by all sentient beings.
The beauty of your name fills the ten directions.

Hearing your name for the first time
Filled me with joy and inspiration.
I traveled, following the stars of the Pleiades in the east.
Not caring what hardships I had to endure,
With great sincerity, I set out in search of you.

Like in the story of *Sadaprarudita*, the Ever-Crying Bodhisattva,
Throughout the trials of my journey
I cried out with yearning heart,
'Oh, when will I meet you, Jetsun Guru?'
When I reached a place one and a half days journey from here,
My body and prana grew so weak that I nearly died,
And I lay in the road like a discarded stone.

But because of my intense devotion and unvanquished will,
Like that of the Bodhisattva Sadaprarudita,
Who met his guru, Dharodgata at Gandhavati in the east,
I was able to complete my journey
And meet you, Jetsun Guru, my father,
At the wondrous place called Fortune Hill.

When I first saw you I got goose bumps,
And my hair stood on end in delight.
No words could describe my joy,
As my longing to see you was at last fulfilled.
Although I had little illusory wealth to offer you,
I had great disgust for samsara,
I had fear of the endless toil of birth and death,
I had renounced all worldly dharmas,
And from the depths of my being, I desired only to practice, to
    meditate.

You accepted me, Jetsun Guru,
And embraced me with your compassion!
I have not forgotten this kindness,
It is branded in my mind.
Please, my Jetsun Guru, always remember me,
And embrace me with your compassion!

Lord Guru, please listen now to your servant,
Who has something to report to you this morning.

At dusk last night I recited the yidam's mantra.
At midnight I prayed to you, Jetsun Guru.
Later, I practiced the meditation on life prana.
Then, just before dawn, I fell asleep,
And free from my ordinary habitual thought patterns,
These wondrous dreams arose:

I dreamed I wore a white long-pointed summer hat.
On its brim, the hat was trimmed with multicolored silken tassels,
Adorned with vermilion fur along its edge,
And with a vulture's feather at the point.

I dreamed I wore stainless new blue-green boots,
Well cut, with four rings and studs of brass,
And fastened with two straps with rings of silver.

I dreamed I wore a white silk shirt,
Embroidered with pearls and golden thread,
And a beautiful design of vermilion dots.

I dreamed I wore a sash around my waist
Made of cloth from *Mon*,
Embroidered with various fine multicolored flowers,
And fringed with tassels and garlands of pearls.

I dreamed I wore around my neck
A cape of white uncut kid's felt,
Fastened with silver jasmine-style ornaments.

I dreamed I held in my right hand
A long strong staff of sandalwood,
Its handle, golden filigree lattice-work,
Inlaid with seven precious stones.
I dreamed I held in my left hand
A vajra skull-cup, filled up
Brimful with golden *amrita*.
Then I felt, 'I want to use
This as my personal drinking cup.'

I dreamed of multi-colored tsampa bags,
Filled with two loads of white rice.
Then I thought, 'I will use
This for my Dharma provisions,'
And slung them over my right shoulder.

I dreamed I wore a black antelope's pelt,
With head and all four hooves intact.
I then said, 'I want to use
This as my meditation mat,'
And slung it over my left shoulder.

Looking to the right I saw
A beautiful golden grassy meadow,
Where many sheep and yaks were grazing.
Then in my dream I strongly felt,
'I want to watch them like their shepherd.'

Then looking to the left I saw
A meadow covered with beautiful turquoise-blue grass,
Filled with many kinds of colored flowers,
And many beautiful women who bowed to me.

In the center of this meadow,
In a garden of countless lovely yellow flowers,
Grew a huge golden lotus,
Where I sat in *bodhisattva posture*.
I dreamed that before me a water fountain flowed,
Behind me a brilliant white aura shone.
My body emanated blazing flames of fire,
And from my heart, sun and moonlight radiated.

These were the wondrous dreams I dreamed.
I know not if the omens were good or bad.
Oh, lord of yogis, knower of the three times,
Please tell me what you make of this.

Thus, Gampopa supplicated Milarepa, requesting him to interpret the amazing omens that had appeared in his dreams.

In reply, Jetsun Milarepa said, "My son, physician monk, do not worry, relax, set your mind at ease. Do not let discursive thinking lead you into the trap of ego-clinging. Let the knots of doubt untie by themselves; cut the strings of dualistic thinking wherever they are thinnest; blow away the dust of habitual thinking wherever it is lightest. Don't stir up your mind by thinking too much, rest your mind in its natural state, effortlessly.

"I am a yogi who has fully mastered the practice of the *illusory body*. Since I have full knowledge and direct realization of the true essence of all dreams as such, I can, of course, interpret dreams, and I can also transform them.[15] Today, I, your old father, will explain the true symbolic meanings of these omens to you. Now give me your full attention, do not let your mind wander, listen carefully to my song."

Then Milarepa sang to Gampopa,

Physician, this is my reply,
Listen closely to what I say.

Son, you have learned Chakrasamvara according to Zang Kar,
And trained in the Kadampa tradition of Upper U.

You have the continuous river of good demeanor,
You have mastered and stabilized good samadhi.
I have always thought you were wonderful and outstanding.
Now, because you thought, 'All these omens are very wondrous,'
You have been caught by your dreams,
And regard them as special.

Son, either you have not learned enough or you are faking.
Have you not studied the many sutras, tantras, and shastras?
In the *Prajnaparamita of True Meaning*
Buddha himself said that dreams are deceptive and are not real,
They are empty, vain, and hollow.
To collect, record, and study them brings little gain.
This is why Buddha used dreams as one of the eight parables,
To show the illusory nature of all things.
Haven't these warnings entered your mind?
Haven't these injunctions occurred to you?

And yet, in this case at least,
Your dreams truly were wondrous omens,
Foretelling marvelous things to come in the future!
I, the yogi who has mastered the art of dreams,
Will interpret their magical meaning for you.
The white long-pointed hat you wore
Shows that just as the point of the hat was very high,
Your tradition and view will transcend the higher and lower
    vehicles.[16]

The silken pleat trim on the brim
Means that you will be adorned with the essence of Dharma,
The subtle yet profound union of wisdom and compassion.

The red and black colors of the fox-fur trim
Are a sign that you will expound on the various teachings
Of the different schools,
Yet will keep them distinct, without mixing them.

The vulture feather on the top
Means that just as the vulture soars to the greatest heights,
You will soar with the realization of Mahamudra, the highest view,
And with vision as keen as the vulture's eye
You will see its stainless unborn essence.

The pair of immaculate Mongol boots you wore
 Is a sign of your exemplary pure and unbroken samaya,
An example for all,
As you progress through the three vehicles.

The 'pair' means that you have gathered
The two accumulations of merit and wisdom.

The four brass studs and color blue
Foretell your attainment of the *four bodies of a Buddha* in this
   lifetime.

The shining silver rings imply
That you'll be free of wrong practices.
You will not act heedlessly nor selfishly,
But like a young prince,
Your actions will be graceful, humble, and considerate,
An example of how a Buddhist should behave.

The white silk shirt you dreamed you wore
Shows that your mind will be free from stain or fault.
The pure gold threads in your lapel
Show your unchanging kindness and good will toward all beings.
The design of red dots means
You'll serve all sentient beings with compassion and skillful means.

The sash you wore of cloth from Mon,
Which wrapped around your waist three times,
Means that you kept and you will purely keep
The vows of all three vehicles,
And that you'll transcend the *three realms*.

The fringe of white flowers, silk, and pearls
Show that you are adorned with the mastery of the three trainings,
And will transmit these by word and example
To your disciples, who will delight in your pure presence.

The cape of uncut white kid's felt
Means that whatever you may be doing,
Your mind will never be separate from
The essential unstained dharmakaya.

The cape being uncut, unstitched, and untailored,
Means that your dharmakaya realization
Is pure, natural, free from doubt, and uncontrived.

The silver clasp that fastened your cape
Is a sign that your realization of dharmakaya
Is a complete realization of unchanging truth,
Not greater nor less than that of Shakyamuni Buddha.

The strong sandalwood staff in your right hand
Means you have found your true and perfect guru.
The seven inlaid precious stones
Symbolize the merits and virtues that adorn your guru.
The golden lattice-work filigree lines on the handle
Are a sign that having received the ear-whispered lineage
   teachings,

You will realize their essence, just as your guru did.
That the lines are interwoven
Means that in the future you will spread
This lineage transmission to many disciples.
Holding it in your right hand
Means that striving forward with great bliss,
You will reach the *Buddha fields*,
As will all those who follow you.

The magnificent vajra *kapala* you held
Signifies the essential emptiness of all dharmas,
And that you will fully realize this emptiness.
Its filling up, brimful, with amrita,
Symbolizes that, filled with great bliss,
You will continuously deepen and increase your realization.
The brilliant golden hue of the amrita
Is the luminosity of all appearances,
And signifies that you will realize this luminosity,
And be able to remain in the natural state of clear light,
Brightening all forms around you.
The desire to use this kapala as your personal drinking cup
Signifies the merging of the previous three delights,
And your attainment of the three *kayas*.
Holding the kapala in your left hand
Shows that these inner experiences will never leave you,
Indeed they will be inseparable from you.

The beautiful multi-colored bags
Show that you will bring your myriad experiences into the path.
Slinging the two bags over your right shoulder
Is a sign that with the provisions of understanding and skillful
    means,
You will travel the Mahayana path.
The white rice inside the bags,
And your thoughts to use it for your Dharma provisions,
Are signs that you will enjoy long life and good health,
And be nourished by the food of meditation.

The black antelope's pelt on your left shoulder
Symbolizes your unwavering mindfulness.
Its head and four hooves still intact
Means that with your perfection of *bodhichitta*,
And your accomplishment of the *four immeasurables*,
You will relieve the suffering and pain of the six realms.
Thinking to use the pelt for your meditation mat

Means that realization has already arisen in you
Through the union of emptiness and compassion,
And will ripen in your followers, too.

The beautiful golden grassy meadow
That you saw off to your right
Shows the increase of both your outer and inner virtues.[17]

The lambs and young yaks grazing there
Are a sign that through your practice of the *four generosities*
You will benefit others and fulfill the wishes of countless beings.
Your wish to watch them like a shepherd
Is a sign that you will protect with kindness and compassion
Those helpless and suffering beings with no protector.

The turquoise blue meadow on your left,
With grass of very even height,
Means that your samadhi will be unshakably steady and pure,
And thus you will taste the state of wisdom and bliss.
The many-colored flowers in bloom
Mean that the many various meditative experiences,
And signs of accomplishment of the different stages of the path,
Will, step by step, arise in you.
The countless attractive women prostrating to you
Means that by keeping pure and unbroken samaya
You will magnetize and master all the dakinis
Dwelling in your channels and drops.

The garden of lovely yellow flowers in the center of the meadow
Means that with your ornaments of realization, strong samadhi,
And perfect observance of discipline,
You will gather great assemblies around you, effortlessly,
Like clouds gather in the sky.

The luxuriant golden 1,000 petaled lotus seat
In the center, above the yellow flowers,
Is a sign that through the superior strength of your wisdom
You will not remain in samsara.
You will rise above the three worlds, unsullied, with pure mind,
Just as a lotus is not sullied in the midst of mud.

Sitting in bodhisattva posture
Is a sign that in the future, because of your great compassion,
You will not rest in nirvana,
But like a youthful bodhisattva,
You will emanate in countless pure forms
To benefit living beings in the six realms,
Who in past lives have all been our very mother.[18]

The water fountain that gushed forth before you
Is a sign that the Dharma will stream from you,
As an ever flowing source, you will spread the kingdom of Dharma.

The brilliant white aura shining behind you
Is a sign that just as the sun gives light and warmth to all,
Your virtue and teaching will purify the land of Tibet.

The great fire blazing from your body
Is a sign that through the blissful wisdom-fire of tummo,
You will melt the ice of discursive thinking.

The sun and moonlight radiating from your heart
Symbolize that you will always remain
In the state of clear light, beyond coming and going.[19]

My son, this dream was very good, not bad.
To prophesy by interpreting signs correctly
Is good, and is allowed in the Dharma.
But in general, it is harmful
To become too attached to dream interpretation.
No matter what experiences you have,
Whether in dreams or while awake, whether good or bad,
If you cling to them as real, they become an obstacle.
If you know that they are but illusion,
You can bring them to the path.

If you do not thoroughly know the art and meaning of dreams,
How can you tell if you have interpreted them accurately?
Some bad omens may appear as good dreams
And only an expert can discern their evil meaning.
However, if you have mastered the practice of dreams,
You can see bad dreams as auspicious and positive.
Generally, dreams are neither good nor bad,
So, son of good family, do not cling to auspicious dreams,
Nor take negative dreams seriously.
Good monk, keep these words in mind.

Thus did Milarepa interpret the magnificent dream of twenty-four auspicious omens, foretelling of Gampopa's illustrious future accomplishments for the benefit of all living beings.

12   Bardo Teachings

In a joyful mood, Milarepa continued, as Gampopa listened attentively.

"My dear son, physician-monk, this was no ordinary dream, it was an auspicious omen for the future. All the signs in your dream predict that the Dharma will flower fully within you. As your old father, I have interpreted for you the symbolic meanings of your dreams in detail, with confidence and omniscient view. Do not forget my predictions, wait and see if they come to pass. When the time comes, when they are verified, a supreme faith toward me will arise in you, far deeper than that which you have now. Then you will realize the effortless true nature of mind in an extraordinary way. At that moment, you will gain liberation from both birth and death.

"But again, I warn you my son: If you want to continue to be a devoted yogi, generally you should never cling to dreams. If you do, you will eventually expose yourself to the influence of the *four maras*. If your dreams are positive, do not have any expectations. If we are filled with hopes and expectations, even positive things can turn negative. If your dreams are negative, don't take them too seriously. Learn to see negative dreams as illusion, not real. Then, although a dream seems negative, because we realize that it isn't real, it becomes a positive thing that prepares us for further development and realization in the spiritual path. This is the practice of a yogi.

"If instead, we disobey the instructions of our guru, if we disregard the sound advice of others, and cling to our self-conceit, then in the long run we will lose our minds and go crazy.

"Furthermore, my dear son, know that this life is merely a part of the bardo of birth-death. All our experiences are unreal, illusory, dream-like. The thought formations we create during our waking daytime hours, create the seeds of habitual mental patterns which transform at night into the myriad delusive visions perceived by our dream consciousness as we sleep. This is the deceptive and magic-like bardo of the dream state.

"When these habitual thoughts become deeply rooted, they drive us into good and bad activities, they create the bardo of samsara, and they compel us continuously to experience pleasure and misery. To purify the seeds of these patterns and end the cycle of samsara, one should practice the dream yoga and the illusory-body yoga. When you master these yogas, you can then realize the *sambhogakaya* in the bardo state. So practice them diligently, my son, until you reach perfection."

Gampopa replied, "Your advice is clear and wonderful, Jetsun. I would do as you say. Can you give me a simple and practical teaching on the different bardos that I might use to carry on this practice and guide me? Then I could apply this wisdom throughout my daily life, day and night."

Milarepa responded in song:

I prostrate to all Jetsun gurus.
I especially take refuge in the kind one
Who bestowed upon me many bounties.
As you have supplicated, my son,
I now sing this Song of the Bardos for you.

All sentient beings throughout samsara,
And all the Buddhas in nirvana,
Are in nature equal, the same in essence.
This is the bardo of view, my son!
The red and white forces in all phenomena,
And the indescribable true nature of mind,
Are inseparable, one in the innate non-differentiated state.
This is the bardo of meditation, my son!

The myriad forms of illusory appearances,
And unborn mind,
Are non-dual, co-emerging.
This is the bardo of action, my son!

Both the dreams you had in last night's sleep,
And the realization of their unreality this morning,
Are one in the light of illusion.
This is the bardo of dream, my son!

The five impure *skandhas*,
And the five pure Buddha families,
Are one in the completion stage yoga of non-discrimination.
This is the bardo of generation and completion stage yoga,
This is the bardo of path, my son!

The father tantras that arise from skillful means,
And the mother tantras that arise from wisdom,
Are one in the third initiation of coemergence.
This is the bardo of heart-essence, my son!

The unchanging dharmakaya that benefits oneself,
And the unobstructed rupakaya that benefits others,
Are but one in the primordial innate state.
This is the bardo of the trikaya, my son!

Birth from the womb of the impure illusory body,
And birth from the pure form of a god,
Are one in the luminosity of the bardo.
This is the bardo of fruition, my son!

Thus Milarepa sang.

13 Dreams, Songs, and Empowerment

After singing his Song of the Bardos to Gampopa, Jetsun Milarepa called all of his close yogi disciples to him. He said to Gampopa, Rechungpa, and Shiwa Ö, "Pay close attention to your dreams tonight. Be sure to remember them. I want you to report them to me tomorrow, and I will interpret them for you."

The next morning, Shiwa Ö arrived first, and told Milarepa, "Jetsun! Last night I had a very good dream. I dreamt that a warm sun shone forth in the east and entered into my heart!"

Rechungpa came next, and said to the guru, "Jetsun! I had a very good dream last night, too. I dreamt that I arrived at three big valleys and shouted in a loud voice."

After hearing these accounts, Gampopa reluctantly came forward. Crying tears of remorse, he said to Milarepa, "I had a very bad dream."

Milarepa replied, "We do not know whether it was good or bad. Don't jump to conclusions. Tell us what you dreamt."

Wiping the tears from his eyes, Gampopa said, "Well, I dreamt that I slaughtered many, many people of many different races. I stopped their breath. Oh, I must be a very sinful person! I must have horrible karma indeed!" And with that, Gampopa burst into tears again, sobbing uncontrollably.

Milarepa smiled to him and said kindly, "Dear son, don't cry so bitterly. Here, give me your hand." Saying this, he took Gampopa's hand in his and continued.

"Son, you will accomplish what you have longed for! Many sentient beings will place their hopes in you for their deliverance from samsara. They will not be disappointed, and their wishes will be fulfilled.

"My son is born! Now this old father has done his share in serving the Dharma!"

Then, turning to the others, Milarepa said, "Shiwa Ö, your dream was only a fair one. Because your commitment to serve the Dharma was not great, you will not benefit many sentient beings. Nonetheless, you will be able to go to the pure land of Buddha Amitabha at death.

"Rechungpa, because you fell under evil influences and violated my injunctions three times, you will reincarnate three more times, in three different valleys, as Buddhist scholars whose fame will be renowned far and wide."

The Dharma Lord Gampopa then returned to his practice and meditated diligently for another month. At the end of the month the faces of the seven *Medicine Buddhas* appeared to him. At that time he needed to breathe in and out only once a day. When he stopped the meditation on the inner winds and exhaled, the visions immediately disappeared.

One afternoon, when he meditated and held his breath, he saw the limitless sambhogakaya buddha-fields, with their infinite wonders. As he experienced these enjoyments, he became distracted and amazed by the marvelous scenes, and let out his breath. Suddenly he found that it was already evening. He thought of telling his guru, but was afraid that he might disturb Milarepa's meditation, so he did not go that evening. Instead, thinking that he might have created obstacles in the meditation, he made mandala offerings to accumulate merit and purify his errors, and he also said many prayers.

At dawn he meditated and again held his breath. This time he saw the faces of the thousand Buddhas surrounding Buddha Shakyamuni. When he went to Milarepa to make obeisance and recount his experiences, the guru said, "You need not tell me of your visions. I already know them. Now you have seen both the *nirmanakaya* and the sambhogakaya sphere of your yidam. You have not yet seen the dharmakaya sphere, but that will happen soon.

"My son, although you would like to stay here with me, because of the vows you have made in previous lives, you must now go to Central Tibet. So, go and meditate there, you have my blessings.

"I have dispelled all of the dangerous obstacles that you have met with in your meditations thus far. Nonetheless, you will soon walk the dangerous path of siddhi. This level of attainment is full of obstacles, for once you have achieved these siddhis, the mara of the son of the gods will come to you. At that time, you should be very cautious, and be particularly careful to keep these powers secret.

"Generally speaking, tantra is an esoteric teaching reserved for superior disciples, and accomplishment in tantric practice must also be developed in secrecy. Following the commitments carefully, a gifted disciple of highly developed capacity will not be influenced by this mara, and as you are clearly a superior being, no mara can ever deceive you.

"Now, for the sake of benefitting all sentient beings, the time has come for you to begin to gather disciples and teach them."

Gampopa was not quite sure that he was ready, and asked his teacher, "When will I be certain that it is the right time to gather disciples?"

Milarepa replied, "You can start to teach and spread the Dharma when you see the true nature of mind, and stabilize that realization. It is true that you have already experienced some realization, but in time you will see your mind essence even more clearly. That will be quite a different experience from those you are having now. Then you will see me, your guru, as the perfect Buddha himself, and a deep and unshakable conviction will grow in you. Then you will be ready to teach.

"The yogi who can bring his inner winds to the tips of his fingers and send them out through his fingertips, can then overcome all the prana-hindrances. Are you able to do this yet, my son? Try! See if you can!"

Early that evening Gampopa piled a heap of ashes on a slab of stone. He retained his breath, charged his fingers with prana, and pointed at the heap. Nothing happened.

Undaunted, he persisted without a break. Darkness fell, the moon rose, and still the ashes did not stir. Then, at midnight, as Gampopa pointed his fingers with intense concentration, the ashes began to move slightly. Gampopa began to grasp the technique, and soon the ashes were swirling around in a circle as if a whirlwind were sweeping them away!

The next morning Gampopa went to see Milarepa, and joyfully recounted his experience of the night before. Mila said to him, "Good! You have not yet completely mastered the pranas, you have only partially controlled them. However, you have now channeled your prana properly, and so you need no longer stay here with me. Soon you will attain both the ordinary and supreme siddhis, and will perform miraculous transformations.

"Now, east of here there is a place by the name of *Gampo Dar*. There you will see a huge mountain that resembles a king sitting on his throne. Its peak looks like an ornamented crown, like the hat I am wearing. The woods and meadows are arranged like a golden mandala. It is surrounded by seven mountains: in front lies a mountain shaped like the precious jewel in the center of the mandala, and surrounding this are six other mountains that appear like six ministers prostrating before the king. On the shoulder of the king-like mountain, Gampo Dar, you will find your disciples. Go there now, and benefit them!"

Then Milarepa sang,

> O monk, are you going to central Tibet?
> My son, when you go to central Tibet,
> At times you may yearn for food.
> Whenever thoughts of food arise,
> Enjoy the food of meditation.
> Realize that all delicious tastes are illusion.
> Experience whatever arises as the dharmakaya.
>
> At times you may feel cold and yearn for warm clothes.
> Whenever thoughts of clothing arise,
> Clothe yourself in the blissful heat of tummo.
> See soft and fine things as illusion.
> Experience whatever arises as the dharmakaya.
>
> At times you may yearn for your native land.
> Whenever thoughts of homeland arise,
> See your true home as *dharmata*.
> Recognize all homelands as illusion.
> Experience whatever arises as the dharmakaya.
>
> Sometimes you may feel poor and yearn for wealth.
> Whenever thoughts of gems and money arise,
> Take the *seven aryan riches* as your treasure.
> Recognize all wealth and possessions as illusion.
> Experience whatever arises as the dharmakaya.
>
> Sometimes you'll feel lonely and yearn for companionship.
> Whenever thoughts of companionship arise,
> Enjoy self-existing wisdom as your companion.
> Recognize all companions and friends as illusion.
> Experience whatever arises as the dharmakaya.
>
> Sometimes you'll miss your guru.
> Whenever thoughts of the guru arise,
> Pray to him as inseparable from you, at your crown.
> Meditate on him at the center of your heart.

Pray to him, never forgetting him.
But recognize that even your guru is a dream-like illusion.
Yes, recognize everything as illusion.
Gampo Dar, the mountain in the east,
Is like a king sitting upon his throne.
The mountain behind is like a hanging white silk scarf.
The mountain in front is like a heap of jewels.
The peak is like a jeweled crown.

Surrounding it are seven mountains,
Bowing like ministers before the king.
The woods and meadows are like a golden mandala.
On the shoulder you will find your disciples.
Go there, son, and benefit beings.
Go, and work for the benefit of others.

Thus Milarepa sang. Then he continued, "I now give you the name, World-Renowned Vajra-Holder Monk."

Milarepa then gave him all the empowerments, teachings, and blessings that the guru possessed. Then he gave him a golden *arura* and blessed it with his tongue and saliva. He also presented Gampopa with a fire-starting kit and tinder-pouch as a farewell gift, and said to his disciple, as a father speaks to his beloved son, "Now, return to your homeland of central Tibet and meditate there!"

14 Final Instructions and Farewell

Gampopa packed up his few belongings, and went to say goodbye to his fellow yogi disciples. Sebenrepa, Rechungpa, Shiwa Ö, and the others all came out to meet him. They were sad to see him go. His sincere dedication and rapid accomplishment had been an unexpected inspiration to them all. Gampopa's example had fired a new enthusiasm in them, pushing them to new levels of accomplishment. Now a light was going out of their lives, and as they each hugged him goodbye, it was clear that Gampopa would be sorely missed. Still, they knew enough about impermanence to take the loss in stride, and they were happy in the certainty that their yogi-brother, "the monk," was on his way to greater things yet.

Now fully prepared to depart for central Tibet, Gampopa went to say farewell to his guru. Milarepa met him along the path and said, "I will see you off, my son. I will escort you as far as Shamboche. There are a few more teachings I wish to give you."

And so they walked together for awhile, father and son. The morning air was fresh and warm, and the sky was cloudless and clear. A gentle breeze stirred the spring mountain flower blossoms as Milarepa and Gampopa walked along the eastern path.

When they came to a stone bridge, the guru said, "My dear monk from U, as a good omen, let us not cross the river together. Here, now, put down your load and let us, father and son, talk for awhile."

And so they sat down beside the river. Mila then took Gampopa's hand and said, "My dear monk from U, stay free of pride and self-centeredness. Cut the bonds of affection and attachment. Abandon all worldly desires for this life. These are the things a good Buddhist yogi should do. Merge all the teachings into one practice: always pray to me.

"My son, do not fall in with those in whom the three poisons of greed, hatred, and ignorance are strong, lest they influence you with their poison.

"There are people who are so full of anger that they see nothing but other's faults, and take all to be their enemies. They heap abuse on others, criticize the Dharma, and are a bad influence on everyone, for in the depths of their hearts, the fires of hatred and anger are always burning.

"To give an example, the snake has neither wings, nor legs, nor hands. Logically it should be a feeble, meek creature. But as soon as anyone sees it, he is seized with abhorrence and fear. This reflects the great hatred that exists within the snake. He who cherishes hatred within will see all men as his enemies.

"And again, some people are very greedy, they grasp and store up everything, even if it is only an old piece of wood or a handful of pebbles. They say, 'When we grow old, we will need some means of provision. When we die, we will need food for offerings in the cemetery.' They insist that one cannot practice the Dharma without money, that even a bodhisattva needs money to accumulate his spiritual provisions. Then they engage in usury and all forms of profit seeking. Their blood is always boiling with greed.

"And again, some people will say, 'Now is not the time for us to practice the transcendental teachings. One should never stick to one teaching, or he'll wind up bigoted, fanatical, and narrow minded. Besides, it is impossible to achieve Buddhahood in one lifetime.' He who does not cultivate bodhichitta will fall into the *shravaka* path. These people are veiled with great ignorance. You should never have dealings with them or pay attention to their babbling.

"If you talk with them, they will first ask you who your teacher is, and what kind of teaching you practice. If you tell them, they will become angry, hate the teachings and the teacher, give up all attempt to practice, and will eventually be reborn in the hell realms. Because of their narrowness, good advice will never benefit them, but will only provoke their wrath. In other words, one's good advice only causes some people to accumulate more negative karma.

"That is why you should stay away from people who are dominated strongly by the three poisons of hatred, greed, and ignorance.

"In the tantric *samayas*, it says,

> To stay more than seven days with shravakas,
> Brings a tantric yogi more harm than benefit.[20]

"In general, you should be full of mindfulness, like a tiny cautious sparrow or a wounded deer. Do not let yourself grow prideful over your discipline, lest you poison all the merit you have gained. Be kindly to every being and in harmony with all. Be peaceful, compassionate, patient, and live purely. You should bridle your wandering thoughts, and avoid the temptation of distractions and idle chatter. You should dwell instead in quiet mountain retreats, seldom leaving your meditation seat. Spend your time furthering your three trainings.

"Although you may realize that your own mind is the Buddha and the true guru, never abandon your guru, the vajra master.

"Although you may realize that all deeds are naturally pure, always practice even the smallest accumulation of merit and do not neglect purification.

"Although you may perfectly realize the emptiness of karma, its causes and results, avoid committing even the smallest negative action.

"Although you may experience the inseparability of the meditation and post-meditation states, continue to practice guru yoga during the four meditation sessions of the day.

"Although you may realize the equality of self and others, do not disparage other teachings or people.

"Son, on the fourteenth day of the Horse month[21] in the year of the Rabbit,[22] you should come to see me. On that day, you should arrive at the border of Drin and Nyenam. Now listen to my song of farewell:

> My son, when ultimate reality beyond description
> Appears in your mind,
> Do not be tempted to engage in sophistries,
> Lest you become proud,
> And get caught up in the eight worldly dharmas.
> Son, rest in humility, free from arrogance.
> Do you understand this, monk from U?
> Do you understand this, physician from Dakpo?
>
> My son, when self-liberation arises within,
> Do not be tempted to engage in logical speculation,
> Lest you waste yourself in useless exertion.
> Son, rest in the state free from discursive thought.
> Do you understand this, monk from U?
> Do you understand this, physician from Dakpo?
> When you realize the empty nature of mind,
> Do not get caught up in ideas of one or many,
> Lest you fall into the extreme of nihilism.

Son, rest at ease in the sphere of simplicity,
Beyond words.
Do you understand this, monk from U?
Do you understand this, physician from Dakpo?

When you practice Mahamudra,
Do not busy yourself in practicing your daily rituals
Of virtuous deeds with body and speech,
Lest the wisdom of non-distinction vanish.
Son, rest in the unfabricated innate nature of mind.
Do you understand this, monk from U?
Do you understand this, physician from Dakpo?

When revelations, visions and prophecies arise,
Do not fixate and grow prideful or overjoyed,
Lest the prophecies become presages of Mara.
Son, rest at ease, in the state of clinging to nothing.
Do you understand this, monk from U?
Do you understand this, physician from Dakpo?

When you see penetratingly into your own mind,
Do not yearn for higher perceptions,
Lest you be caught by the Maras
Of desire, joy, and pride.
Son, rest at ease in the state free from hope.
Do you understand this, monk from U?
Do you understand this, physician from Dakpo?

Then Milarepa placed his feet upon the crown of Gampopa's head, and said, "Noble monk from U, I have just imparted to you all the four initiations. Now be happy! Be full of joy!" Thus, in words, song, and gesture, Jetsun Milarepa conferred upon Gampopa the four initiations.

The act of putting his feet upon Gampopa's head symbolized that in addition to the other initiations, Milarepa had given his disciple the vajra guru empowerment, which authorized Gampopa as a *vajracharya*. He also gave Gampopa the initiation of expression-samadhi, and then said, "I have an unusually profound pith-instruction, but it is too precious to just give away. I am through now, son. You may go."

Milarepa then embraced Gampopa and bid him farewell on his journey. Gampopa hoisted his pack and crossed the stone bridge, leaving Milarepa standing back on the other side of the river. Gampopa knew that Milarepa had already transmitted all his lineage teachings, and wondered what this more profound doctrine could be. He continued walking east, but when he reached a distance barely within earshot of

where Milarepa still stood, he heard his guru calling him. Turning, he saw Jetsun Milarepa, quite far away now, motioning him to come back. Puzzled, Gampopa walked back, and again crossed the stone bridge to see what it was his guru wanted.

His eyes burning brightly, Milarepa said to him, "Who else but you deserves to receive this most precious quintessential instruction, even though it be of too great a value to be given away? Now come here, and I will give it to you!"

Gampopa was overjoyed, and asked, "Should I first offer you a mandala?"

"No, it is not necessary for you to offer me a mandala. I only ask that you will cherish this teaching, and never waste it."

He then led Gampopa behind a large nearby rock.

"Now look!" Milarepa said, and hoisted the back of his robe, revealing the cheeks of his buttocks, all covered with lumps of hard callus, like the hooves of an animal, due to having sat for so long on stony ground without a cushion. He said, "There is no more profound teaching than this. Now you can imagine the hardships I have undergone. My attainment of great realization came from this.

"It has simply been due to persistent effort that I have accumulated merit and gained accomplishment. You need such effort, not any other doctrine. This is the essence of my teaching. Whether you become a Buddha or not depends on effort. With it, there can be no question about your liberation. Like a son, do what your father says!

"You should likewise continue to exert yourself with great perseverance in your meditation. You should continue sitting on one seat, in one place, until you attain realization. This is the most profound teaching in Buddhism: Practice!"

This teaching made an indelible impression on Gampopa, giving him inspiration and courage on many occasions thereafter.

Gampopa expressed his heartfelt gratitude to Milarepa, and thus, on that sunny, clear spring morning, father and son parted.

After Milarepa had seen Gampopa off, he returned to Chuwar, gathered all his disciples together, and said to them, "This physician-monk who just left will benefit countless sentient beings. Last night, I dreamed that a vulture flew from here to Ü, and landed on top of a great mountain.

"From all directions countless flocks of geese gathered round. After a while they dispersed in different directions, and each goose gathered five hundred attendant geese. Thus all the plains and valleys of Tibet became white with geese.

"This dream means that, although I am a yogi, many of the followers of my lineage will be monks. This physician-monk will carry on my lineage, and will benefit innumerable sentient beings."

Milarepa continued with heartfelt conviction and joy, "Oh, my good disciples, I, your old teacher, am happy beyond words! I have now completed my service to the Dharma, and have fulfilled the prophesies of the Buddha!"

15 The Death of Milarepa

Gampopa left Milarepa and journeyed on foot until he reached central Tibet. Upon his arrival there, he went first to visit his old Kadampa teacher, Geshe Nyugrumpa. Still dusty from his long journey, Gampopa was shown into his former teacher's quarters. Geshe Nyugrumpa was joyful to see his old student again, and immediately noticed the signs of spiritual attainment radiating from the monk before him. When he learned that Gampopa had been studying under the renowned mountain yogi Milarepa, Geshe Nyugrumpa asked, "What kind of virtues have you attained?"

Gampopa replied, "My prana does not escape from within, and my realization is as vast as space."

Nyugrumpa was moved. He offered tea to Gampopa, and invited him to stay at the monastery, but Gampopa had other plans. He accepted his teacher's hospitality for a few days only, just enough time to rest and restore himself after his long trip. Then he said goodbye and set off for Rolka, to meditate in solitude. After remaining in Rolka for some time, he journeyed to Nyel, and continued his practice there with great focus and discipline.

After staying at Nyel for a while, he remembered his guru's parting instructions, "Son, on the fourteenth day of the Horse month in the year of the Rabbit, you should come to see me. On that day, you should arrive at the border of Drin and Nyenam."

To Gampopa's dismay, the appointed time had already passed. Nevertheless, he borrowed twelve ounces of gold from his friend, Gyapasare, and left the next morning. On the way he stopped to ask Regomrepa, a fellow disciple of Milarepa who was meditating in a nearby cave, to accompany him as his traveling companion. Regomrepa readily agreed, and the next morning the two set off together.

Proceeding toward Chuwar, Gampopa had gotten as far as the Yarlung Valley, when he met Milarepa's heart-disciple, Rechungpa. Rechungpa told him the sad news that Jetsun Milarepa had entered into parinirvana on the fourteenth day of the Horse month, and then handed Gampopa his share of Milarepa's sacred treasures, such as his aloe-wood staff, and the hat of the *Acharya* Maitripa.

Gampopa was overcome. He cried out in anguish, shed many tears, and then fainted. Rechungpa and Regomrepa threw water on his face and massaged his hands and feet to revive him. After a short time he regained his senses, but continued weeping in his grief. Then rising, he drew eight ounces of gold from his purse and scattered it as an offering in the direction of Drin and Nyenam. Gampopa then sang this song of prayer and supplication to his guru:

> Jetsun, when you stand at the summit of the white snow
>   mountain,
> Your deeds are like a white snow lioness,
> You are the yogi who conquers the views of others.
>
> Jetsun, when you go into the forest,
> Your actions are like the striped tiger.
> You are the yogi who is free from hope and fear.
>
> Jetsun, when you go to the white rock peak,
> Your way is that of the white vulture.
> You are the yogi who has conquered space.
>
> Jetsun, when you wander without a care in mountain solitude,
> Your path is like that of a wild animal.
> You are the yogi who is free from attachment.
> Jetsun, whose actions are like an elephant's,
> You are truly beyond meditation and post-meditation.
>
> Jetsun, whose actions are childlike,
> You are truly free from inhibition.
>
> Jetsun, whose actions are beyond concepts,
> You have truly realized dharmata.
>
> Jetsun, since you have the highest perceptions,
> You have truly merged your inner mind with luminosity.
>
> Jetsun, whose thoughts for food or drink are slight,
> You truly enjoy the food of samadhi.

Jetsun, like the wish-fulfilling gem,
Whatever one needs, one receives from you.

Jetsun, like the full moon among a sky full of stars,
You are the most lovely among many.

Jetsun, like the lotus rising above the mud,
You are unstained by the faults of samsara.

You are very kind and compassionate to all beings.
You have accomplished the wishes of the Kagyu.

Your virtuous qualities are without measure,
And my praise is but a trifle.

Hold me close with your compassion, and accept me.
Even though I have no material gifts of veneration to offer,
I will practice
Until we become one in the dharmakaya.
Do not cease your river of blessings.
Do not let me go from the iron hook of your kindness.

Through the virtue of these praises,
May I meet the Jetsun himself.
When we meet, please grant your blessings.

Thus Gampopa sang, with tears of deep devotion. After a while, having recovered himself, Gampopa invited Rechungpa to return with him to his own home in Nyel. Rechungpa accepted, and they made the journey home together. On the way, Rechungpa told Gampopa and Regomrepa the miraculous details of Milarepa's death. He spoke of how, after Milarepa's cremation, all the disciples who were present when the guru died left for their mountain solitude, intending to spend their whole lives in meditation retreat, in accordance with his instructions. This news heartened and inspired Gampopa.

Once they had returned, Rechungpa gave Gampopa the complete instructions for the higher esoteric meditations on the yidam Chakrasamvara. Gampopa also received his share of Milarepa's cotton robe, and many other Dharma teachings as well. Then Rechungpa said farewell, and left for the monastery of Loro Dol. It was later told that, having transformed his earthly body into the sambhogakaya, Rechungpa finally merged into the all-embracing emptiness.

Soon after these events, Gampopa met a beautiful and wealthy young female patroness, who promised to sponsor his meditation practice. Thus he stayed for six years at Sewalung in Nyel, and for seven years at Gelung in Rolka. In those places he meditated as continuously as a river flows.[23]

One night, while Gampopa was meditating in a place called Sup, he dreamt that he had a son. In the dream, he cut off his son's head and cried, "I have cut off my family line." He then rolled the boy's corpse down a hill. Thereafter, he had no further dreams, and his sleep was always an experience of the luminosity of clear light.

Finally Gampopa came to realize the true nature of mind, and the full meaning of his guru's words. He saw that all of samsara and nirvana are but dreams and illusions. Thus he attained the wisdom free from elaboration. He realized that this was his last birth in samsara, and thought, "This is like returning home, effortless."

Then Gampopa sang,

> I sing a song of the *dharmadhatu* of great bliss.
> I speak these words in the state of wisdom,
> And thus resolve the truth of non-duality.
>
> This compassion, that benefits others, free from attachment,
> Seize it firmly as supreme skillful means.
>
> This *innate coemergent awareness*,
> Seize it firmly as wisdom.
> When certainty arises, it is this.
>
> These discursive thoughts of fixation,
> Seize them firmly as the dharmakaya.
> When one experiences this, one sees the essence.
> Sights and sounds, the habitual patterns of labeling,
> Seize these firmly as the ultimate truth.
> When certainty arises, it is this.
>
> These discursive thoughts are the origin of fixation.
> When one masters this, one sees the truth.
> If one wishes to realize this truth,
> Practice continuously, like a river.
> Rest loosely, without additional fabrications.
> Rest naturally, without seeking any further.
> Rest easily, without thought.
>
> Experience and realization are one.
> When realization is uninterrupted, that is it.
> When it is as boundless as space, that is it.
> When one sees one's mind as Buddha, that is it.
>
> Now I have realized the true dharmata.
> Fixation has been self-liberated.
> Without thinking, I have spontaneously accomplished realization.
>
> This is not common, and it is not for the common ones.
> Great learning cannot understand this.

Great knowledge cannot know this.
Discursive thinking cannot label this.

I stay on the path of blessings.
I follow the words of the guru.
Those who are faithful will achieve realization.
Is your realization like this, all you great meditators?
This should not be told to everyone.

Thus, as his guru had predicted, at this time Gampopa fully realized his lama's great kindness toward him, and saw Milarepa as the Buddha himself. Thereafter he had no increase nor decrease in realization, nor any acceptance, rejection, nor doubt.[24]

16 Daklha Gampo

After his illumination, Gampopa meditated for seven years in Rolka. Many people began to gather around him, and presented heaps of offerings to him. Gampopa needed little, and distributed the offerings among his neighbors, the people of Rolka.

When the warm weather of summer came, he went to Ode Kungyal Mountain, to enjoy meditation in its quiet and magnificently beautiful atmosphere. One day, as he was meditating at dawn, he heard a voice in the sky saying, "Neglecting to benefit beings is the downfall of the bodhisattva."

Taking these words to heart, Gampopa thought, "I should leave this solitude immediately and begin to share the Dharma with others." However, before he could even begin to gather his few belongings and set out, a man appeared in the guise of a king, wearing a crown and a huge turquoise around his neck. The king promised to care for Gampopa's needs if Gampopa would simply stay on the mountain. The king then added that if Gampopa chose not to stay, he should go on to Gampo Dar, where the king's own son would care for Gampopa's needs.

"I am a sky-flying hungry ghost," the king said. "Though I do not mean to harm others, nonetheless many suffer because of me. I hereby confess to you all my evil deeds, and ask that you give me refuge ordination and the bodhisattva vow."

In answer to the ghost-king's earnest plea, Gampopa gave him the purification method of the *four powers*, teachings on compassion, refuge ordination, the bodhisattva vow, and instructions on Mahamudra. Having received these, the ghost-king thanked Gampopa, and then disappeared into thin air like a rainbow.

Gampopa decided to go directly to Gampo Dar. Arriving there, Gampopa was awestruck by its natural splendor. Gampo Dar and the mountains of Daklha Gampo were the most spectacularly beautiful countryside that he had ever seen.

Deeply inspired, he decided to build a retreat house at Sanglung. He intended to do a twelve year retreat, with the hope of achieving the state of being able to transform the essences of the five elements directly into nourishment. However, scarcely had he completed his retreat house, when a lady smeared with ashes and holding three peacock feathers appeared before him, and said, "It is more important to cause the teachings to flourish now, than it is for you to enter into a long retreat." After saying these words to him, the lady vanished.

As he was preparing to enter into retreat a few days later, two learned Buddhist monks, Geshe Gyalwa Chungtsang Chen and Geshe Nyanak Marpo, came to seek audience with Gampopa. Gampopa was obliged to meet with them, and give them teachings, even though it delayed his retreat. Soon after that, sixty more disciples gathered around him. After giving teachings to these earnest men, Gampopa again planned to enter into strict retreat. However, so many sincere disciples, proper vessels for the Dharma, streamed in from U, Tsang, Kham, and elsewhere, that he was obliged to remain outside retreat and give teachings to them all.

Before long, as prophesied by the Guru Milarepa, and by the Victorious One, Shakyamuni Buddha, no fewer than 51,600 disciples gathered in the rocky mountains of Daklha Gampo, to study at the feet of the Dharma Lord Gampopa. Five hundred of these were like *arhats*, and among the other experienced disciples who came, many were to achieve realization of the teachings, mastery over the channels, winds, and drops, and attainment of the *six psychic powers*. These disciples would not accept any form of support without first checking whether it had come from one of the eight impure sources. They adopted the twelve ascetic disciplines, and meditated continuously, not even pausing to lie down.

Never before in the history of Tibet had so many Dharma students assembled at one time.

17 The Three Yogis of Kham

Among the 51,600 disciples gathered around Gampopa, who out-wardly obeyed the code of the *Vinaya* and inwardly practiced the *two stages of yoga*, the three yogis of Kham were the highest.

One of these three Khampas was from Dege, and his name was Dorje Gyalpo, or Dorgyal for short. Dorgyal was an emanation of Shakyamuni Buddha himself, coming in fulfillment of the Buddha's promise to support Gampopa in spreading the Dharma. In this life-time Dorgyal was a fully ordained monk, who had already studied under many great lamas and received many teachings and em-powerments from the Kadampas, the Sakyapas, the Naropa lineage, and several other traditions.

At the age of twenty-nine, hearing of Gampopa, Dorgyal came to see the famous guru at Daklha Gampo. Upon meeting Dakpo Lhaje, Dorgyal saw him as the embodiment of all Buddhas, and prostrated humbly before him. He offered a mandala with strong and pure devo-tion. He wept from the core of his being, and in that moment an ex-traordinary faith was kindled in his heart and mind. Opening com-pletely to the guru, he told Gampopa of his life and his meditation experiences.

Gampopa replied, "You seem to think that your attainment is great." Then, holding out a handful of barley, Gampopa continued, "This is greater!"

At that, all of Dorgyal's previous *shamatha* experience vanished! Gampopa then said, "Now sit on that rock and concentrate on your mind, without creating a form."

Dorgyal obeyed, and in that sitting actualized the meaning of Mahamudra. In that instant, a rainbow appeared, bridging the space between Dorgyal and Gampopa, and Dorgyal realized without error the heart-essence of all of the Buddha's teachings.[25] After that, Dorgyal remained at Daklha Gampo, and later became known as the great Phagmo Drupa.

The second of the three Khampas was from Do Kham, and was known as U Se, or "gray head," as he was born with gray hair. U Se was an emanation of Avalokiteshvara, the bodhisattva of compassion. He was later to become known as the Karmapa, or "Man of Buddha Activity," prophesied in the *Samadhi-raja Sutra*, coming to help Gampopa spread the Dharma. In this lifetime, U Se was also a fully ordained monk, instructed in the Dharma from childhood by his parents, who were themselves accomplished practitioners. U Se entered the monastic community at sixteen, and was fully ordained at twenty. At this time he studied the Vinaya, the Kalachakra teachings of the Kadampa, and the Lam Dre teachings of the Indian Mahasiddha Virupa.

The fame of the Dharma Lord Gampopa reached U Se's ears at the age of thirty, and he traveled to Daklha Gampo to meet the great guru. When they met, Gampopa instructed U Se in the Lam Rim of the Kadampas as a preliminary practice, and told U Se to practice it as he himself had done. Later, having given him this basic training in the sutrayana approach, Gampopa gave U Se the empowerment of the yidam Hevajra. During the initiation ceremony, U Se saw that Gampopa had actually become the body of light of Hevajra.

A little later, on the advice of Gampopa, U Se entered a shamatha meditation retreat for nine months. Throughout the duration of his retreat, so dedicated was U Se, that he never unfolded his hands long enough for the perspiration on them to dry. His extraordinary diligence did not escape the notice of his guru, who recognized U Se as one of his most gifted disciples. Thereafter Gampopa instructed him in advanced *vipashyana* meditation. U Se practiced this for three years until he began to attain siddhis. His development of insight was like the sun dispelling the clouds of ignorance. At this time Gampopa told him, "You have cut your bonds with phenomenal existence. Now you will not return to samsara."

The third Khampa was from Nangchen, and his name was *Saltong Shogum*.

Except for the three Khampas, all the rest of the disciples kept the monastic discipline of the Vinaya very purely. The three Khampas appeared very wild by contrast, as they did not maintain the monastic discipline. They did not have to, for they were all highly realized beings, and their actions were beyond any negativity.

In order to practice the tantric ceremony of the ganachakra feast properly, they requested of Gampopa over and over again to be allowed to drink alcohol.[26] One day, when they were living at Boulders Like Horses and Yaks, Saltong Shogum said to his two Khampa companions, "We are of the lineage of the Mahasiddha Naropa. We must practice the twenty-fifth day celebration of Dakini Day. Wouldn't it be wonderful to do a Vajrayogini ganachakra this next Dakini Day?"

Dorgyal replied, "It certainly would, but here in the community we are bound by the drinking rule. If the head disciplinary monk catches us, we will be punished."

However, Saltong Shogum was not to be discouraged, so they deliberated among themselves over what they should do to celebrate the upcoming Dakini Day on the twenty-fifth day in the first month of the summer. They continued to make their request of Gampopa, until finally the guru relented and gave them each permission to make a *chang* offering from three skull cups of barley. Together they took their nine skull cups full of barley and brewed up some very delicious beer.

On Dakini Day they took the beer up to a beautiful spot on a nearby mountain. They also brought with them all of the other sacred substances necessary for the ganachakra. Then they demonstrated their siddhis and performed miraculous acts to show that the beer could not affect them. Dorgyal of Dege herded and chased logs for the fire as if they were animals, driving them up the hill with his slingshot, and the logs ran from him as if in terror. U Se of Do Kham carried water for their meal up the hill in a fishnet. Saltong Shogum of Nangchen started their cooking fire by sending forth wind from the fingertips of one hand and fire from the tips of the other.

They had a great day on top of the mountain. In the evening they performed the Vajrayogini sadhana in a spirit of exhilaration and bliss. They drank beer, performed miracles, sang many doha songs and danced the sacred offering dances. They even performed the great Kagyu folk dance, with its secret song of supplication:

> On this day, let us vajra brothers supplicate,
> Let us truly supplicate and blessings will enter.

> You who dwell on a sun and moon seat on the crown of my head,
> Kind Root Lama, I supplicate you.

> In the Dharma palace of Akanishta,
> Great dharmakaya Vajradhara, I supplicate you.

In the east, in the precious monastery of Sahor,
Tilo Prajnabhadra, I supplicate you.

In the north, in the monastery of Pushpahari,
Learned Mahapandita Naropa, I supplicate you.

In the south, in the monastery of Drowo valley,
Translator Marpa, I supplicate you.

In the highland pasture of the Lachi snow mountains,
Lord Mila Laughing Vajra, I supplicate you.

In the east, in glorious Daklha Gampo,
Dharma King, Physician from Dakpo, I supplicate you.

In the west, in the palace of Uddiyana,
Consort Vajrayogini, I supplicate you.

In the charnel grounds of Cool Grove,
Dharmapalas, Mahakala, Mahakali, I supplicate you.

May inner and outer obstacles not arise.
Please grant me the ordinary and supreme siddhis.

Thus they supplicated with many songs and much dancing. They were still very excited and in high spirits as they returned home, singing doha songs and dancing as they entered the monastery compound. The head disciplinary monk heard them, and he was greatly annoyed, for singing and dancing were not permitted in the monastery. He came out and beat the three Khampas with a stick, saying, "You three have broken the law of the *sangha*! Singing and dancing go against our traditions and violate Dharma law. You cannot stay here anymore. You must leave this monastery immediately!"

Still in a state of transcendent elation, Dorgyal sang to the monk in reply, "The ground is the field of equanimity...," explaining to the disciplinarian how to drink beer, but the monk policeman would not listen, and growled, "You must leave tonight!"

Seeing that the disciplinary monk did not understand, Dorgyal asked that they be allowed to stay the night, for it was already dark, and promised that if they were permitted to stay the night, they would leave the next morning.

"All right. You can stay the night, but tomorrow morning, as soon as it's light enough to see the road, all three of you be off!"

So, before dawn broke the next morning, the three yogis of Kham left the monastery. Each had time only to gather up what few belongings he had, and then they were shown the door. They were ushered out so early and so brusquely that they did not even have time to

prostrate to their guru, Gampopa, nor to ask his permission to leave. As the monastery was high up on a mountain, they set out down the mountain toward the valley below.

At that time, Gampopa was not in the monastery, but was meditating in a retreat hut further up the mountain. At the moment that the yogis left, he remarked to his attendant, Lord Gomtsul, "Last night I had a vision that great and wondrous miracles were taking place in the streets of the monastery. But this morning, the *dakas* and dakinis are preparing to leave! Nephew, please look outside, and see if anything has happened to the three yogis of Kham."

Lord Gomtsul stepped out the door of the retreat hut to find out what was happening. Looking down the mountain, he saw the three yogis of Kham already way down the valley at Prostration Ridge, the point at which the monastery could first be seen, and where approaching pilgrims would prostrate toward the monastery. There, the three yogis of Kham were making their final prostrations of respect to Gampopa, since the disciplinarian had not allowed them to do so at the monastery before they left.

Lord Gomtsul then noticed that the birds were chirping louder than usual, and looking up, he saw that all the birds were flying away from the mountain toward the valley where the three yogis were. Not only were the dakas and dakinis leaving, not only were the birds leaving, but Gomtsul saw that even all the grass and trees were bending in the direction of the yogis, as if they wanted to uproot themselves and leave the mountain, too! All this Lord Gomtsul saw, and all this he reported to the precious guru, Gampopa.

Gampopa said, "This is not good! The three men of Kham must have been punished by the disciplinarian. This should not have been done!

"For many kalpas, those three Khampas have accumulated merit and purified their obscurations. How can any ordinary person pass judgement on their behavior or understand the quality of their meditative experiences? Our ability to gather here at Daklha Gampo is the result of past commitments and prayers made during the time of Shakyamuni Buddha. They should definitely stay here for the time being. If the disciplinary monk has sent them away, I feel like leaving, too! I am going to go after them, and tell them to come back up!"

So saying, Gampopa left his hermitage at Sewa cave, and walked briskly down the southeast side of the grassy mountain, behind the western hill, where he finally caught sight of the three Khampas in a steep ravine. The guru then climbed to the top of a large granite boulder, grasped the corner of his monk's robes with his hand, and signalling with his other hand, he called to his three disciples to return, singing:

Ka ye! Listen, my three highest heart sons!
Sons, don't go any further down. Come back up!

Many lifetimes ago
We had a deeply auspicious and profound karmic connection.
In the presence of the Lord Sambuddha, the *Bhagavan*,
The protector Shakyamuni,
When I was the young Bodhisattva Chandraprabha,
I supplicated and was granted the *Samadhi-raja Sutra*.
You were the leaders of the vajra brothers,
Who gathered there in a retinue of many tens of thousands.

The Tathagata then spoke these words:
'In the future, when the dark age has come,
Whoever spreads the meaning
Of this profound Dharma, the *Samadhi-raja Sutra*,
Will be the son of all the Buddhas of the three times.
He will be the best of physicians, curing all sickness of the kleshas.
How the Victors will praise him is beyond words.'

When he said this repeatedly, again and again to everyone,
I promised to spread that teaching,
And all those assembled there
Also made aspirations and promises to help me.
Because of our excellent past aspiration, we have met again in
    this time.
Those sharing in that karma and merit are very fortunate.
We were taught well in that profound Dharma,
And now we are established in the stage of non-returning.
Sons, don't go any further down, come back up!

This excellent spot, this sacred Gampo mountain,
Is the palace of the ocean of divine yidams.
The great meditators who practice in this place
Quickly attain the ordinary and supreme siddhis.
Sons, don't go any further down, come back up!

I am the father guru, the great meditator Nyiwa,
The trustworthy spiritual friend.
The disciple-sons who rely on me
Quickly realize the Dharma of Mahamudra.
Sons, don't go any further down, come back up!

The disciples who properly follow the guru's word
Will certainly benefit greatly,
In this life and the next.
There is no reason to doubt, have confidence.
Let faith arise in your hearts, you fortunate ones.
Sons, don't go any further down, come back up!

The yogic discipline of secret actions is your ally.
Maintaining your practice throughout the four periods of the day,
Your heartfelt longing of devotion
Is the supreme friend who speeds you along the path.
Sons, don't go any further down, come back up!

Generally, your vajra brothers and sisters, these companions,
Are people who act in accord with the Dharma,
And practice the highest meaning of Mahayana.
There are no better friends than these.
Sons, don't go any further down, come back up!

The profound Dharma, the *six dharmas of Mahamudra*,
Is the essence of the sutras and tantras, the heart of the Buddha's
    teachings.
Those who wish to be liberated
Will not find instructions superior to this pith.
Sons, don't go any further down, come back up!

If you know how to practice without error,
All the paths and *bhumis* will be traveled simultaneously.[27]
Fruition will actually manifest in this life.
How satisfying, not to be held back until next life!
Sons, don't go any further down, come back up!

A good place to practice, a spiritual friend, good companions,
And Dharma that speeds you along the path,
You could find nothing nobler than these four,
No matter where you searched.
Sons, don't go any further down, come back up!

If you forsake these four paths, where will you go?
Now that we have met through such positive and auspicious
    coincidence,
Do not think too much about hope and fear.
It would be good for you to practice longer in this place.
Sons, don't go any further down, come back up!

From the Dharma palace of Akanishta,
This is the command of the dharmakaya, great Vajradhara:
Come back, up and up!

Thus Gampopa sang, a song thenceforth known as "Sho mo! Come back up!" With such conviction and fervor did the Dharma Lord Gampopa make this command, that he left the imprint of his two feet and his staff on the boulder where he stood.

The three men of Kham saw the guru arrive and signal with his hand, and heard clearly his song. They were overjoyed, and prostrated to him many times. From the top of the boulder where they stood, down in the ravine, they offered him a joyful doha song and sacred dance in response:

In the Dharma palace of Akanishta,
Dwells great Vajradhara.
So, on this occasion, let the vajra brothers make this supplication:
The guru has said, 'Come back.' So we are going back, up and up,
We are climbing the steps of the higher realms, going up and up.
We are stamping down the lower realms, going up and up.
Sho mo! What a joyful, good experience!

In the east, in the precious monastery of Sahor,
Dwells Tilopa Prajñabhadra.
So, on this occasion, let the vajra brothers make this supplication:
The guru has said, 'Come back.' So we are going back, up and up,
We are climbing the steps of the higher realms, going up and up.
We are stamping down the lower realms, going up and up.
Sho mo! What a joyful, good experience!

In the north, in the monastery of Pushpahari,
Dwells learned Mahapandita Naropa.
So, on this occasion, let the vajra brothers make this supplication:
The guru has said, 'Come back.' So we are going back, up and up,
We are climbing the steps of the higher realms, going up and up.
We are stamping down the lower realms, going up and up.
Sho mo! What a joyful, good experience!

In the south, in the monastery of Drowo valley,
Dwells Marpa the Translator.
So, on this occasion, let the vajra brothers make this supplication:
The guru has said, 'Come back.' So we are going back, up and up,
We are climbing the steps of the higher realms, going up and up.
We are stamping down the lower realms, going up and up.
Sho mo! What a joyful, good experience!

In the highland pasture of the Lachi snow mountains,
Dwells Lord Milarepa Laughing Vajra.
So, on this occasion, let the vajra brothers make this supplication:
The guru has said, 'Come back.' So we are going back, up and up,
We are climbing the steps of the higher realms, going up and up.

We are stamping down the lower realms, going up and up.
Sho mo! What a joyful, good experience!

In the east, in glorious Daklha Gampo,
Dwells Dharma Lord Gampopa, the Physician of Dakpo.
So, on this occasion, let the vajra brothers make this supplication:
The guru has said, 'Come back.' So we are going back, up and up,
We are climbing the steps of the higher realms, going up and up.
We are stamping down the lower realms, going up and up.
Sho mo! What a joyful, good experience!

Thus sang the three yogis of Kham, and their dancing left many footprints in the rock as well. Their song of response came to be known thereafter as "Sho mo! Going back up!"

Then, master and heart-son disciples went back up together to the monastery at Daklha Gampo. After that, the community had no further ill feelings toward the unusual behavior of the three Khampas. Lord Gampopa continued to live in Sewa Cave above the monastery, while Dorgyal lived in the Khyunding Cave, U Se lived in Tsekar Cave, and Saltong Shogum lived in Chumik Cave. These three yogis of Kham vied with the yogi Chojung and other accomplished ones in the signs of a siddha. In time, each of them came to further spread and expand the glorious teachings of the stainless practice lineage.

18 Stories of the Master Gampopa

Having established a thriving monastic community, hosting tens of thousands of worthy ordained monks and yogi disciples, Gampopa spent the rest of his life at Daklha Gampo. There, as abbot and guru, he divided his time between his personal meditation retreats and teaching his many diligent disciples.

By this time Gampopa had reached the highest level of the Mahamudra path, and as his guru, Jetsun Milarepa, had prophesied, he had attained both the ordinary and extraordinary siddhis: miraculous powers and ultimate realization of the true nature of mind. His displays of wisdom and compassion, and his performance of many wondrous miracles, were witnessed by many people. What follows is a sampling of the aphorisms, inspiring stories, and teachings from this period of fruition in the guru's life.

* * *

A very simple fellow, who was also a student of Gampopa's, did a brisk trade in religious texts, images, and other religious objects. He went to Gampopa and asked how to purify this sin. Gampopa told him, "You must earn again as much profit as you have made in this way, and use that profit to build a temple."

The simple fellow worked hard to establish a temple, complete with beautiful images and other works of art, but the task soon became troublesome; it was so time-consuming that it left him with no chance to meditate.

He returned to Lord Gampopa and said, "I am spending so much time acquiring images and books for the temple that I am distracted, and can find no opportunity to meditate."

His guru told him,

"If you can sustain an understanding of dharmata for even a moment, this will purify a whole mountain of non-virtue."

* * *

Gampopa said, "Generally, I had great difficulty in giving rise to meditation experience within my being. Now it seems that all of you give rise to it without difficulty. In addition to the profound path of skillful means of the oral instructions, the transmission of blessings is the specialty of the Kagyus, and is without equal."

* * *

Gampopa said, "When you first begin to practice, you must be like a deer locked in a pen, or a prisoner in jail, urgently seeking a way out of samsara.

"In the intermediate stages of practice, you must be like a farmer during the harvest. Once he has determined that it is time to reap his crop, he works at it continuously, no matter what anyone tells him. Just as a farmer works to make the most of the crop he has grown, we who now have opportunities and conditions which are so valuable to our practice, should use them immediately, understanding that there is no time to be wasted.

"In the final stages of practice, you should be like someone whose work is drawing to a close, and who is looking forward to the time when he can put it aside and dwell at ease.

"With regard to how much time there is for practice, you should be like someone who has just been hit by an arrow and who is trying to get rid of it. He does not bother about who shot it or where it came from—he just acts swiftly to remove it.

"When you meditate, you should be like a mother who has lost her only child, but its image is still with her, whatever she is doing. Then, in the later stages of practice, which are concerned with realizing emptiness--the final nature of all phenomena--you should be like a herdsman who has brought all his beasts home. He has had much to watch for and cope with, but now they are all home safely, and he feels relaxed, his mind is free.

"If you repeatedly meditate on impermanence, attraction for the things of this life will be lessened. This will make it easy for the Buddhas to bestow blessings on you. If you achieve great realization of impermanence, the Buddhas will appear to you and foretell your future lives, including the one in which you will complete the path."

* * *

Gampopa manifested in innumerable forms. The people at Daklha Gampo reported that on the thirteenth day of the twelfth month he went to Lhasa, on the fourteenth day he prepared a ceremony, on the fifteenth day he made flower offerings, on the sixteenth day he did the closing prayer offerings, making offerings to other monks, and on the seventeenth day he returned to Daklha Gampo Monastery, bringing with him many sacred texts, as well as barley, butter, and wool cloth. There he made dedication prayers.

However, his patron, Gebum, and his retinue, requested that Gampopa come to visit them at the same time. Thus, on the fourteenth day, Gampopa made preparations, on the fifteenth he made flower offerings, and on the sixteenth he recited the concluding prayers. Then, along with seven monks, he flew up into the air, to the wonderment of all. Many offerings were made to the monastery, for which Gampopa did the dedication of merit.

At the same time, the monks who were in retreat declared that on the thirteenth day Gampopa came out of his retreat, that on the fourteenth day he gave instructions to the monks from Tsang, on the fifteenth he gave teachings to the monks from Kham, and on the sixteenth day he gave teachings to the monks from Ü. Thus, the group of retreat monks declared that the precious guru had never left the area at all!

However, three of Gampopa's attendants, Selchang, Shegom Ghangseng, and Gompa Lengtse, all said that during this same time the Lama Gampopa gave no teachings, neither did he leave the area, nor did he eat the offerings, but instead sat in solitary retreat!

* * *

One time Gampopa's attendant, Gompa Lengtse, remarked to Gampopa, "In the past, the shravakas achieved great states of samadhi, such as the overpowering contemplative manifestation, the all-encompassing contemplative manifestation, and others. How did they attain this?"

Gampopa replied, "If one practices, there is no reason why someone cannot achieve these states today."

One morning after this conversation, when Gompa Lengtse went to the lama's room to make an offering of yogurt mixed with sugar, he saw a great fire in the center of the room, with flames blazing up to the ceiling. Terrified, he ran from the room shouting for Selchang, another attendant, to come quickly.

When they returned to the room, the lama had transformed the fire into the all-encompassing contemplative manifestation, and in this state was simply sitting peacefully on his meditation seat.

Another time, Gompa Lengtse went into the shrine room to make a butter lamp offering, and found the place filled with water.

"What is happening here?" he cried in wonderment.

Then he heard the voice of the lama call out, "Come here."

And so saying, Gompa Lengtse saw the lama transform the water into the all-encompassing contemplative manifestation.

* * *

On yet another occasion, Gompa Lengtse went into Gampopa's room bearing a torma offering, planning to receive the Chod teaching which cuts the four maras. Not seeing the lama there, he went and looked outside, but found no sign of the lama there either. Then he heard Gampopa's voice calling out, "What do you want? Come here!"

And instantly, the lama appeared, sitting in his usual place of meditation!

* * *

One time, when the lama was staying in a room high up in the monastery, the patron Gyalson arrived, and asked the attendant if he might be able to see Gampopa and present offerings to him. When the attendant entered the lama's room to check, he did not see the lama, but in the center of the room he saw a golden stupa, radiating brilliant light. The attendant rushed back to Gyalson, hoping to show him this marvelous appearance, but when the two returned to Gampopa's room, they found only the lama sitting there.

* * *

Once, Lord Phagmo Drupa said to Lopon Gompa, "Have you noticed that Je Gampopa casts no shadow?"

Lopon Gompa had not, so that night, when Gampopa was standing before a butter lamp, Lopon Gompa looked, and saw that indeed

Gampopa cast no shadow. Later, during the day, when the lama was standing in the bright warm sunlight, Lopon Gompa checked again, and noted that still the Lama cast no shadow.

* * *

Once, when Gompa Lodro arrived to make an offering of one hundred thousand leaves of paper, he received permission to enter Gampopa's room. Entering, he saw the form of the thousand-armed Chenrezig. He returned to Gampopa's attendants and asked who had built so marvelous a statue, and where he might find Gampopa. Puzzled, the attendant Gompa Lengtse led him back to the lama's room, where they found Gampopa seated in the spot previously occupied by the thousand-armed Chenrezig. No sign of the statue was to be found.

* * *

One time, all of the monks in retreat decided to make a great offering to the lama. They built a giant throne and made tea and food for everyone. When Gompa Sheson went to get the lama and escort him to the feast, Gampopa gave him his outer yellow teaching robe and told him to go on ahead. Then Gampopa closed the room door. Waiting nearby, Gompa Sheson looked toward the shrine, and to his shock, saw that the lama was already seated upon the throne! When he entered the shrine room, the monks asked him, "Why did you not precede the lama and take care of his robe?"

* * *

On another occasion, Lama Gompa remarked to Gampopa, "A bodhisattva who has achieved the first bhumi can demonstrate miraculous powers by placing the three thousand universes into the smallest dust particle. The dust particle does not grow bigger, neither do the three thousand universes grow smaller, yet the one fits into the other.[28] How wonderful this is!"

Gampopa replied, "This is the nature of phenomena. Anything can be achieved. The small eyes of human beings can see the whole of a face. The four inches of a mirror can reflect horses and elephants. A small bowl of water can hold the entire moon. Now look at me!"

When Lama Gompa looked, he saw that the lama had transformed himself into a huge Buddha, as large as the entire mountain of Daklha Gampo, yet he fit into a room that normally held only five people. The room had grown no larger, nor had his body grown smaller.

* * *

One time, when the sun was in eclipse, a thousand monks in the monastery saw Lama Gampopa flying in the sky and sprinkling water from a vase.

* * *

Another time, Gargom Karpo requested that Lord Gampopa give the transmission of the thirteen yidam deities. The lama agreed, and as he was reciting the *mala* mantra of the thirteen deities, a red light issued from his mouth and dissolved into Gargom. Gargom felt great devotion, and began doing prostrations to the lama. As soon as he began, the lama manifested as the four-faced, twelve-armed yidam, Chakrasamvara.

* * *

Once, on behalf of his mother, Kyogom produced a thangka of the five buddha families. He asked the guru, Gampopa, to bless it quickly.

Gampopa agreed, saying, "Burn this stick of incense and make a mandala offering."

He then transformed himself into the Buddha, and from his *ushnisha* there radiated a glorious light that dissolved into the thangka. The air resounded with the tinkling of bells and the drumbeat of the *damaru*, and the sky was filled with parasols, auspicious banners, and canopies. The sound of cymbals was heard, and a rain of flowers fell from the sky.

When Kyogom saw this, the lama said, "This is the way to do a rapid consecration."

* * *

Once, Geshe Gyalwa Chungtsang Chen thought to himself, "The precious lama does not permit the novice monks to do anything but meditation, so how can they possibly acquire knowledge?"

That night, he dreamed that the entire mountain was transformed into caves, and in each cave there was a precious stupa, beautifully carved and radiating light. Many people were doing prostrations before them, saying that they were the refuge of all beings in samsara, including the gods.

The next morning, he went to Gampopa's room to tell the lama of his dream, but before he had time to recount it the lama said, "Generally, those who rely on intellect hate me, and have contempt for me. My novice monks are exactly like the stupas you saw in your dream. These beggar children are the refuge of all the sentient beings in the six realms of samsara, including the gods.

"I can encompass the needs of all, high and low. Some say that I am causing the teachings to decline, but if you watch closely, those who benefit from the Buddha's teachings will be well known in the years to come."

* * *

Radzi Gomkye became adept at meditation merely by hearing the lama's name. Although Gyasom Dorseng did not actually see the lama, he nonetheless mastered meditation through his devotion and mandala offerings to Gampopa. Innumerable disciples, such as Nampa Phenne and others, achieved meditative concentration merely by seeing Lama Gampopa's face.

* * *

Once Rukom asked, "When one achieves the state of *one taste*, do body, mind and appearance become one?"

Gampopa demonstrated by waving his hand through a pillar, and replied, "Just as there are no obstructions when one moves one's hand in space, so, body, mind, and appearance become one."

* * *

Once, while traveling on his way to Drabkyi Tsali, Gampopa crossed a river on his meditation mat, fingering a mala in his left hand while performing the water *mudra* with his right hand.

* * *

When Gampopa was staying at the mountain of Dregu, the local king, Lhagom, requested that he consecrate a temple there. In response, Gampopa threw a flower into the sky and it dissolved into the shrine.

At the same time, his ritual vase remained in the air, and he hung his robe on a sunbeam. To King Lhagom and the others gathered there, Gampopa then appeared in the form of Chenrezig Khasarpani.

* * *

When he was staying at the Yen Phug cave, Gampopa told his attendant, Lengtse, to keep silence for seven days. During this time, the lama repeatedly passed through cave walls without obstruction. He also manifested as a gigantic skeleton, riding a tiger in the sky, with a sword in his right hand, a skull cup in his left, and a *khatvanga* staff by his left shoulder.

* * *

Once Gampopa remained for three days, standing with his heels together and making the joined-thumbs nectar mudra over the crown of his head. On the first night, he appeared in seven forms; on the second night, he appeared in fourteen forms; and on the third night, his many forms filled the entire cave. Then all the forms disappeared.

* * *

Gampopa could remain an entire night breathing in and out only once. Those of his disciples who needed basic instructions, those who needed to dispel obstacles, those who were weak in realization and who needed the teachings to deepen their understanding, all had their wishes fulfilled merely by performing the torma and mandala offerings, and doing yoga exercises. Thus, Gampopa possessed inconceivable and inexpressible qualities, such as the six psychic powers and others. In this way, he was able to benefit countless sentient beings of the past, present, and future, in accordance with their needs.

19 The Parinirvana of Gampopa

When he saw that the end of his mortal life was drawing near, Gampopa said, "I have labored greatly for the Buddha's teaching, and kindled the flame of wisdom in sentient beings who were so blind. Thus, the work that was to be done for those disciples in this life has been done, and for the sake of future generations, I have composed many meaningful texts. I want to assure my disciples, now and to come, that if they rely on me, I will protect them from the sufferings of samsara and birth in the lower realms. Therefore, do not be sad."

In order to demonstrate impermanence to others, this unsurpassable great master, Gampopa Sonam Rinchen, the World Renowned Vajra Holder, the Physician from Dakpo, although free from birth and death, dissolved the mandala of his manifested form, and left his body on the fifteenth day of the sixth month of the Water Bird Year (1153 C.E.), at the age of seventy-seven.

At that time many wondrous and miraculous signs were seen by many beings. Rainbows appeared in the sky, along with parasols, victory banners and canopies; flowers rained down from space, while different kinds of music and celestial singing were heard throughout the land. A delightful smell of indescribably fine incense pervaded the region.

On the eighteenth day of the month, Lord Phagmo Drupa officiated at the cremation and last rites of his beloved guru, Gampopa. When the faithful people from the four directions around Daklha Gampo had gathered for the ceremony, they looked up and saw a rain of blue flowers falling from the sky. When the cremation fire was lit, the earth shook, and five-colored smoke appeared, along with different colored lights and the sound of offering music. These phenomena were seen and heard throughout the entire region of Dakpo.

After the cremation fire had burned down, they found that the lama's heart, symbolizing his love, and his tongue, symbolizing his teachings, had remained untouched by the flames, and many other precious relics were found amidst the ashes, unharmed by the fire and left to be used for accumulating merit for sentient beings.

For three days after the cremation, all the people who had gathered there remained dissolved in the samadhi of great devotion, feeling no need of food or sleep. By the power of the lama's great compassion, all those sentient beings who were connected with him entered onto the path of enlightenment. At the deaths of all those beings connected with him, even if they had been sinful, rainbows appeared and flowers rained down in blessing.

Thus did the manifest earthly life of the great Dharma Lord Gampopa come to a close. The cause of his birth was in fulfillment of his promise to the Buddha Shakyamuni, made sixteen centuries earlier, to help spread the Dharma. Long was his coming foretold in many scriptures, and the brilliance of his great Dharma light still brightens the world today, as the waves of his limitless compassion and penetrating wisdom continue to directly benefit countless sentient beings.

Epilogue

The light of wisdom and love that the guru brought into this world was strong. Through his peerless example and his compassionate teaching, the stainless lineage of the great Dharma Lord Gampopa did not die with him, but was transmitted to many proper Dharma vessels.

Among them were his four supreme disciples—Phagmo Drupa, Dusum Khyenpa, Lopon Gomtsul, his nephew, and Lopon Gomchung; his four great disciples—Lama Shri Phagpa, Sergom Yeshe Nyingpo, Yogi Chojung, and Somching Yeshe Nyingpo; his close disciples— Dampa Kyelpo, Gyatsa Repa, Josey Layakpa, Dakpo Dulzin, Gargom Karpo, and others; and his close attendants—Joden Lengtse, Changye Salchang and, in particular, Badrompa.

Khampa U Se left Daklha Gampo before Gampopa's death. Later, when word reached him that his teacher had died, he returned to Daklha Gampo, where he had a visionary experience of his teacher in the sky. Later, he journeyed to Gampo Nyenang, where he attained enlightenment at age fifty through the dream yoga practice, as his teacher had prophesied.

At the moment of his enlightenment many dakinis gathered and wove a black vajra crown for him out of their hair. This crown is still visible, to those of good karma, above the heads of all the Karmapa incarnations, signifying their realization of the true nature of reality.

Khampa U Se remained at Gampo Nyenang for eighteen years. During that time he built a monastery and retreat center, and attracted many devout disciples. The fame of his realization spread, and he soon became known as Dusum Khyenpa, "Knower of the Three Times," signifying his omniscience through his understanding of the unborn nature of mind. Later, the Kashmiri pandit Shakya Shri identified him as the Karmapa, "the man of Buddha activity," as prophesied by Shakyamuni Buddha in the *Samadhi-raja Sutra*.

Dusum Khyenpa's tradition became known as the Kamtshang or Karma Kagyu tradition, and he subsequently established his principal monastic seat at Tsurphu, which remained the seat of the Karmapas until the Chinese takeover in 1959.

Before his death at the age of eighty-four, Dusum Khyenpa left an envelope stating the particulars of his next rebirth. Thirteen years later, in fulfillment of the terms of his letter, he was reborn and recognized as the second Karmapa, Karma Pakshi. This established the *tulku* tradition in Tibet, which has been emulated by thousands of other enlightened lamas, including the succession of Dalai Lamas.

Gampopa's nephew, Lord Dakpo Gompa Tsultrim Nyingpo (Gomtsul), received the lineage of Gampopa's monastery, Daklha Gampo, and continued the lineage known as the Dakpo Kagyu tradition. This later became known as the Tsalpa Kagyu, after Gomtsul's spiritual heir, Zhangtsalpa Yudrakpa Tsondru Drakpa.

Gampopa's disciple, Baram Darma Wangchuk, left Daklha Gampo and traveled north to Baram. He settled there and began to teach and give meditation instruction. His tradition became known as the Baram Kagyu tradition.

After Gampopa's death, Khampa Dorgyal (Dorje Gyalpo) remained at Daklha Gampo for a year. Then, as Gampopa had predicted, he went north. Dorgyal found a place in the forest of Kuntuzangpo called Phagmodru, and built a monastery there, under the patronage of the King of Drak Khawa. At Phagmodru he gathered over 80,000 disciples, five hundred of whom attained the level of realization known as "Holding the Golden Umbrella." Thus, he became renowned as the Dharma Lord Phagmo Drupa.

Phagmo Drupa was the most expansive teacher of Gampopa's disciples. From the vastness of the teachings he had collected, he gave different teachings to his various disciples according to their needs, and in so doing, gave rise to eight different traditions, founded by his eight great disciples. Thus he was both the spiritual father of one of the four elder Kagyu lineages (the Phagmodru or Phagdru Kagyu), and the spiritual grandfather of the eight younger Kagyu orders— Drikung, Taklung, Lingre or Drukpa, Yamzang, Trophu, Martshang,

Yelpa, and Shugseb—which were founded by his realized disciples. From these lineages came many great lamas and mahasiddhas.

Gampopa drew his general Dharma teachings, such as the Lojong or Seven Points of Mind Training, and the Four Thoughts Which Turn the Mind Toward Religion, from the Kadampa lineage, and transmitted these to his disciples as the foundations for Dharma practice. These teachings he combined with the special instructions on the "Six Yogas of Naropa," and meditations on Mahamudra. Gampopa taught these two traditions to all his disciples.

All of the branches of the Kagyu lineage thus received from their gurus both the Kadampa foundations and the completion stage teachings of the Six Yogas of Naropa, also known as the short path of Mahamudra, to bring worthy disciples to full realization. They then gave different instructions to their various disciples according to their individual capacities and natures, needs, and inclinations. As a result, after Gampopa there arose different traditions within Mahamudra, for example, "The Method of Recognizing the Nature of the Three Kayas of Mahamudra," most favored among the Karma Kagyu; "The Fivefold Profound Path of Mahamudra," emphasized by the Drikung Kagyu; and "The Method of Teaching the Six (or Eight) Factors of One Taste," which is the specialty of the Drukpa Kagyu.

All of these traditions are still alive today, passed on from guru to disciple in an unbroken lineage from the Buddha Vajradhara to the present, a transmission not merely of intellectual understanding, but of true meditative realization. Each of these teachers received the oral teachings from their guru, practiced what they were taught, attained realization, and then out of the greatest kindness and compassion, continued to work for the benefit of all sentient beings. Only by their indefatigable efforts have the teachings come down to us today.

Thus we owe the deepest debt of gratitude to the incomparable Dharma Lord Gampopa, and to all the lineage forefathers, as their aspirations for the liberation of every sentient being continue to bear limitless fruit, even centuries after their earthly demise. By hearing and contemplating the stories of their lives, may we be moved to follow their certain path to Buddhahood. If already on the path, may we be heartened and inspired to renew our efforts, to overcome obstacles as all the gurus most surely did, and to realize supreme enlightenment in one lifetime, for the benefit of all sentient beings.

Colophon

The milk-like ocean of view, meditation, and action,
Is churned into the butter of enlightened wisdom.
I bow to the peerless Gampopa,
Who caused the teachings of the Buddha to flourish,
And united the lineages of the Kadampa and Mahamudra.

The History of the Kagyupa Order

by Lobsang P. Lhalungpa

After completing his training under Milarepa's guidance, Gampopa established the first Kagyupa monastic center in Daklha Gampo, in the southern province of Tibet. It has since been one of the most sacred places of pilgrimage for Tibetans and other Himalayan Buddhists as well. Gampopa used the Kadampa monastic system as the model for his new monastery. Later, all Kagyupa monasteries adopted the same system. Gampopa's devotion to monastic training did not keep him from giving personal guidance and service to both common folks and the growing number of cotton clad repas who, in their contemplative quest in the high mountains, emulated the life and practice of their original master, Milarepa.

Gampopa applied his eclectic background to propagate the Buddhist teachings. He incorporated the Kadampa teachings known as The Stages to Enlightenment (Jangchub Lamrim) and the highly specialized Training of Mind in Bodhichitta (Jangchub Semjong, commonly called Lojong) into the regular Kagyupa training. The latter, as the true essence of Mahayana, is intended for a devotee's development of bodhichitta. It consists of aspiration and application bodhichitta on the relative level and true bodhichitta on the ultimate level.

Gampopa propagated his Kagyupa version of the self-realization system of Mahamudra[29] both orally and through his written works, such as *The Jewel Ornament of Liberation (Lamrim Thargyan)* and *The Four Dharmas (Dakpo'i Chozhi)*. In these writings he compiled both the words of the Buddha and those of the mahasiddhas.

Gampopa also advanced a radical concept, identifying all mental events, good, evil, and neutral, to have one common nature, identical with the ultimate state of reality (dharmakaya). This view is among the points that evoked criticism from some classical scholars of other Buddhist orders.

Mahamudra is usually perceived to be similar to the Chinese Ch'an and the Japanese Zen systems. Both emphasize special reliance on the contemplative process in general, and immediate awakening through direct insight into the primordial state of mind and reality. The sources of Mahamudra and Mahasampanna (Chakchen and Dzogchen) are the Transcendental Wisdom Sutras (Prajnaparamita-sutras) and the *Highest Yoga Tantra* (Anuttara-yoga-tantra). Hence these two self-realization systems are regarded as being authentic.

The Kagyupa Order

The Kagyupa order emerged in Tibet during the eleventh to twelfth centuries C.E. and strengthened the ongoing Buddhist renaissance movement. During the ninth century the destruction of Buddhism and its monastic centers had thrown Tibet into abysmal darkness for seventy-five years. In 836 the Buddhist King Tri Ralpachan was assassinated by supporters of his disgruntled elder brother, Lang Darma, who then proclaimed himself king. As part of his revenge, Lang Darma carried out a thorough religious persecution. But before long the apostate king himself fell at the hands of the Buddhist monk Lhalung Paldor in 842. This event triggered an internecine fight between the royal heirs which ended in both princes fleeing to remote parts of the country. Thus the central dynastic rule of Tibet came to an end, and Tibet fell under the domain of petty rulers and tribal chiefs.

However, this politically chaotic situation proved to be favorable to the Buddhist revival. Buddhists hiding from persecution quietly paved the way for the difficult renaissance. In isolated areas of eastern and western Tibet the monastic system was re-established, while the esoteric order of the Nyingmapa, the oldest school—established during the eighth century—re-emerged, albeit in a somewhat transformed state and with hardly any organizational base. In due time, and without any opposition from the adherents of the native Bon religion, most of the principalities became patrons of different Buddhist orders.

The Kagyupas contributed much to Buddhism's revival and expansion. The effective vehicles for these achievements were their stable monastic centers, the institution of reincarnate lamas (tulkus), and the cave-dwelling or wandering *yogins* and *yoginis*. Kagyupa teachers, writers, poets, and artisans also played a vital role in the development of Tibet's religious tradition and culture.

The Kagyupa order is a loose conglomerate of monastic centers, each of which functions independently, while remaining loyal to the common history and heritage—rather like a necklace with many strings. This is in contrast to its sister order, the Gelugpa, which maintains a homogeneous character with a single institutional entity and functional coherence—somewhat like a stringed instrument.

The term Kagyupa means "Adherents of the Secret Oral Transmission." The syllable *ka* stands for "oral teachings"; *gyu* for "transmission" (from teacher to disciple—originally restricted to a one-to-one relationship); the *pa* means "adherents". Sometimes, however, *ka* (spelled *bKa*) was pronounced as *kar* (spelled *dKar*), which means "white robe", and originated from the white cotton robe worn by the Kagyupa saint Milarepa during his years as a hermit.

As the monastic centers of various Kagyupa schools multiplied, so did their lay devotees all across the country. During the early stage of Kagyu history, four large orders (called "elder") and eight small orders (called "younger") were established. The Kagyupas, like other schools, were the creation of individual Tibetan teachers. These independent orders were generally influenced by the personalities and preferences of their respective founders. By maintaining and passing on to disciples the distinct practices of self-realization taught by their founders, the unique traditions of the various lineages were upheld.

The immediate source of the Kagyupa esoteric teachings were the mahasiddhas (the "Great Realized Ones"), the wandering ascetic teachers of the Indian subcontinent. They were widely recognized and highly revered for their wisdom, miraculous powers, and their complete detachment from any materialistic and selfish concerns. Often they were called "crazy yogins" on account of their unconventional behavior, stunning wit and wisdom, and carefree life-style. Their life stories and songs (dohas) challenge institutional and individual corruption and confusion. The best known amongst the Tibetan crazy yogins is Drukpa Kunley. Born in 1455, he was supposed to have lived to 115 years of age.

Principal among a host of Indian mahasiddhas were Tilopa, Maitripa, Naropa, and Savaripa, all of whom lived during the tenth to twelfth centuries. These, together with their predecessors, constitute the "blessing lineage of self-realization practices." The earlier line of teachers included the exalted Asanga, Saraha ("the Sovereign of all Realized Ones") and Nagarjuna, and was linked all the way back to the historical Buddha.

The Kagyupa orders also deeply revere the Tibetan teachers of the blessing lineage. In addition to Gampopa, their adherents revere Marpa and Milarepa. These three are seen as the paramount founders who established the Kagyupa esoteric tradition in eleventh and twelfth century Tibet.

Ngawang Namgyal Taklung (1142-1210), founder of the Taklung Kagyu school, sums up the common and special self-realization practices of various Kagyupa orders as follows: "In summary, they maintain as their foundation the yearning for spiritual liberation of the arhat vehicle (*Hinayana*), the compassionate motivation of the bodhisattva vehicle (Mahayana), and the extraordinary commitment of the secret mantra vehicle (*Vajrayana*)."

They also uphold their own distinct self-realization systems, such as the oral elucidation of the tantras introduced by Marpa and Ngok, the perseverance of Milarepa (Nyingru), Gampopa's Clarification of the True Reality (Ngowo'i Gyedar), and others.[30] The significance for practitioners lies in the fact that each practice embodies the others in a harmonious way, and that each reveals the one essence as encompassing all realities, and all realities being ingrained in one essence!

Marpa

Marpa (1012-1097) was the Tibetan founder of the Kagyupa esoteric system. He was a teacher of high attainment with penetrating insight into the hidden human potential of his disciples. He did not set up a formal Buddhist center, but instead turned his own home into a tutorial center (lama'i zimkhang), a custom which was to become popular throughout Tibet. In addition to general teachings, Marpa gave his disciples many important empowerments and higher esoteric teachings, such as the four secret oral transmissions, which represent an important branch of the Buddhist Highest Yoga Tantra. The four secret oral transmissions consist of the attainment of the illusory body; the luminous clarity of mind and reality; the mastery of dreams (the inner dynamism of stream-consciousness); and the development of inner heat for enhancing the authentic self-realization, characterized as the blissful union of compassion and insight.

Marpa was revered throughout the Tibetan Buddhist world because of his own struggle in the quest of Buddhist teachings, his superb scholarship and high attainment. His learning and mastery of Sanskrit were reflected in his superb translation of many important esoteric texts from Sanskrit into Tibetan. Tibetan scholars hailed him as their sovereign translator.

Marpa's best known disciple was Milarepa, Tibet's great poet-saint. In fact, Marpa's fame was greatly enhanced by his stunning success in carrying out the unconventional training of Milarepa, which led to Milarepa's becoming a highly enlightened teacher himself.

Marpa was married, had children, and lived in the village of Dowolung in the province of Lodrak in southern Tibet. His wife, Dakmema, was very kind and supportive of him. She was an accomplished teacher in her own right but had no wish to assume such a role (although this was done by women teachers at various times in Tibet).

Marpa had an imposing physique, penetrating eyes, and wore his hair long. He also had a domineering personality and was perceived by others to be short tempered and uncivil. In the course of his search for Buddhist teachings he travelled to tropical India three times, across dangerous wilderness areas and under difficult conditions. His followers had collected gold to support his religious mission, which enabled him to travel through various regions of India and study under numerous Indian Buddhist teachers such as Maitripa, Dipankara Atisha, and Naropa. Naropa was to become his most important teacher, guide and illuminator. From him Marpa received many prophetic signals, one of which concerned a future disciple by the name of Milarepa, who "was destined to be a great teacher of mankind." He was to be handled with skill so as to rid him of his temporary spiritual malaise.

Milarepa

Milarepa (1040-1123) was Marpa's foremost disciple and was to become a truly enlightened teacher. He and his younger sister, Peta Gonkyi, were born to a rural family in the Mangyal region of western Tibet.

His early life was filled with tragedy and misery, starting with the death of his father. Before his death, his father had entrusted his earthly possessions to his brother and sister for the care of his widow and two small children. The greedy relatives lost no time, however, in appropriating the land and possessions, while mistreating the unfortunate widow and her children. Reduced to abject poverty, the helpless victims had to struggle for their survival through hard labor and begging. They were shunned by neighbors and friends, and their lives became almost unbearable. Finally, the embittered widow resorted to a desperate scheme of revenge: She sent her young son to a famous master sorcerer in Tsangrong Valley to learn the art of sorcery. In due time, Milarepa mastered the evil practice (which had its origin in the pre-Buddhist culture).

Prodded by his mother, Milarepa started casting powerful spells over the relatives. First, his uncle's house collapsed and killed many of the relatives during a wedding party. Next, their crops were destroyed by a terrific hailstorm. While Milarepa was thrilled with his triumph over his mother's tormentors, the whole village was outraged. But as the whole family began disappearing, Milarepa was overcome with scruples and remorse. The Buddhist principle of personal karma was deeply ingrained in his consciousness. Eventually he felt compelled to seek out certain teachers, who eagerly tried to counsel him but failed. Then he was directed to Marpa, the translator. This marked the turning point in his life.

Marpa knew that this young disciple was predestined to be one of the greatest master-meditators and teachers, but first he had to be completely transformed through a series of harsh ordeals. Therefore, from the start, Marpa treated him roughly. First, he demanded a worthy gift in exchange for the precious teaching he had brought from India at great cost and the risk of his life. Young Mila pleaded for the teachings by telling of his tragic life and his yearning for spiritual solace and liberation. Since he could not raise any significant material gifts, he humbly offered Marpa his whole being: his body, speech, and mind. Marpa thereupon demanded that he build a nine-storied tower. Thus began years of rigorous struggle for the poor disciple.

Milarepa had to manage the entire construction by himself, from digging the foundation to cutting the lumber and constructing the masonry. His ordeal was made even more torturous when, several times, Marpa ordered the construction torn down to be rebuilt at a different site. While Milarepa was suffering from a sore back Marpa would give advanced teachings to his other disciples. When Mila tried, with the help of Marpa's compassionate wife, to quietly sneak in and attend the teachings, he was jeered at and thrown out.

Finally, after more than six years, Milarepa's great moment came. His evil karma was evidently exhausted and its cumulative defilements neutralized just when the tower was about to be completed. Marpa finally accepted him as a disciple and showed fatherly affection towards him, addressing him as "my son." Marpa explained the purpose of the cruel ordeals of the past and assured him that he would pass all the precious teachings on to him like a "gift of heavenly ambrosia poured from one vase into another." He then asked his wife Dakmema to prepare a great feast for the auspicious occasion, following which he empowered Milarepa into the highest order of esoteric Buddhism, and predicted that not only would he achieve true enlightenment, but that he would become the greatest of all teachers. He assured him that he would illuminate innumerable people, including the highly revered ones, and that the Kagyupa teachings would last as long as a great river. He further advised Mila to devote himself completely to contemplative self-realization in the solitude of the high mountains of the Jomo Langmo region.

During the course of his quest, Milarepa devoted all his efforts to meditation. Clad in a simple cotton robe, he let his hair grow long. With only an earthen pot to cook his food and a small bundle of special instructions from Marpa, Milarepa spent many years in different mountain caves. He lived on occasional supplies of roasted barley flour and on nettles from the surrounding slopes. His determination and devotion to the contemplative practice were so complete and unwavering that he rarely descended for food.

His practice started with the conquest of the self (the egoistic delusion) and progressed to developing the noble thought of enlightenment (bodhichitta) and an unlimited aspiration for universal well-being and enlightenment. After mastering the various aspects of the self-realization system as revealed by the Buddhist Supreme Yoga, Milarepa then concentrated on the vital essence, i.e. the activation and diffusion of supernormal heat (tummo). His control of this ecstatic thermal power was largely responsible for his survival. He thus attained complete control over his body and mind. In addition, he gained imperturbable tranquility, tolerance, sensitivity, compassion, and wisdom.

Even before meeting Marpa, Milarepa was convinced that an authentic contemplative practice with full devotion is the most reliable, if not the only, means of self-realization and enlightenment. Yet he never imposed his personal conviction and commitment to the contemplative path as the only self-realization process. Both during his mountain solitude and after his spectacular self-transformation, this incomparable meditator and master guided innumerable men and women with skill and compassion. In doing so he followed the Buddha's characteristic approach by teaching each individual according to his or her needs, temperament, will, and spiritual potential, which is generally hidden in the individual's stream-consciousness.

Milarepa's life of asceticism and retreat were in sharp contrast to the external life of his teacher, Marpa. When Milarepa was asked why he did not follow Marpa's example externally, he answered that for him to do so would be like a hare trying to follow the steps of a lion. And, when one of his disciples asked, "Can we engage in an active life as long as it proves beneficial to other beings?" Milarepa answered, "If there is no attachment to selfish aims, you can. But that is difficult."

If Milarepa's attainment was regarded as comparable to that of the great teachers in the higher echelons, his subsequent ministry and its impact were no less astounding. He transformed men and women of diverse persuasions into beings of higher moral maturity, tranquility, and self-realization. His own sister, Peta Gonkyi, became one of his highly advanced women disciples. The achievement of these ordinary disciples was especially impressive, since they were not products of a complex monastic education and thorough training. Other independent, non-monastic disciples of Milarepa were to emulate him by becoming cotton-clad, long-haired "Repas", who would spend almost their entire life in contemplative solitude in high mountains, or wander around villages and towns in Tibet singing the message of Milarepa to ordinary folk.

One of his learned and realized disciples, Rechung, quietly propagated Milarepa's teachings, especially the advanced self-realization system associated with the meditation deity Chakrasamvara. Gampopa, possibly the most learned monk among his disciples, was chosen by Milarepa to become the dharma regent in order to preserve and promote the Kagyupa teachings.

Ever since the turn of the century Milarepa's life story has been known in the West and interest in him continues up to this day. His life story is available in many languages. The "Collected Songs of

Milarepa," now available in English, complement his life story (although the translation of his works as "The Hundred Thousand Songs" should not be taken literally). Milarepa's poetry shows refreshing lucidity and simplicity, enlivened with witty folk idioms. The latter were popular with common people in Tibet who had little formal education but were well versed in the rich oral tradition and figurative expressions.

Milarepa was so popular a teacher that he became a folk hero. Anecdotes of his life were enacted in classical and folk plays throughout Tibet. The high mountain cave where he had lived and the nine-storied tower he built were among the sacred places of pilgrimage until destroyed by Chinese Red Guards in the 1960's. In the entire Tibetan Buddhist world Milarepa is hailed as the greatest meditation master and sovereign of the realized ones. He became a legendary figure in his lifetime and has fascinated people ever since. The lineage of Marpa and Milarepa is looked upon by all orders as the source of authentic blessings and guidance, and their self-realization practice is considered to be particularly effective for attaining inner solace and enlightenment.

The Dakpo Kagyu: The Origin of Most Kagyu Branches

As entrusted by his principal teacher, Milarepa, Gampopa very successfully carried out the task of propagating the Buddhadharma in Tibet. He made a great contribution toward advancing the Buddhist renaissance which began during the end of the tenth century. While Gampopa was actively propagating Buddhism the population of learned monks and meditators steadily rose. Among his disciples, according to the Kagyupa hagiography, were about five hundred highly attained monk disciples and eight hundred great meditation masters, not counting the many ordinary followers. Each of his four outstanding "spiritual sons" established an independent monastic center. Karmapa Dusum Khyenpa founded the Karmapa Order; Phagdru Dorje Gyalpo established the Phagdru Order; Baram Darma Wangchuk founded the Baram Order; and Zhang Tselpa Tsondru Dragpa established the Tselpa Order. Other sub-schools later came into being as offshoots of the first two. All of the branches stemming from Gampopa are collectively referred to as the Dakpo Kagyu, since Dakpo Lhaje or Gampopa is their common spiritual ancestor.

The Karma Kagyu Order

One of Gampopa's principal disciples was the aforementioned Karmapa Dusum Khyenpa (1110-1193). He developed into such a highly accomplished and revered teacher himself that he became a legend in his lifetime. Apparently the preeminence he achieved in learning, humanistic endeavors, and enlightenment was the result of his extraordinary spiritual power.

He was born a child prodigy to devout Buddhist parents. Once his father had blessed him with the transmission of a sacred mantra he started his Buddhist studies and practices under various lamas, many of whom were of the older Kadampa Order. Later, under the guidance of his principal teacher, Gampopa, Karmapa devoted years to meditation in the solitude of mountain caves and hermitages, which led him to a higher realization.

Karmapa became famous as a great saint with extraordinary spiritual powers. He is said to have benefitted numerous individuals by healing the sick, deformed, blind, depressed, and disturbed, while guiding others towards realizing their goals. His preeminence was reflected in his vision of destiny and personal mission for the distant future.

Karmapa created the Karmapa (or Karma Kagyu) Order when he established the first monastery in the Tsurphu area, some thirty miles west of Lhasa, and subsequent monasteries in Kham, eastern Tibet.

His personal name, Karmapa, came to mean "a person of manifold activities." This indicated a person with a bodhisattva's attainment who accomplishes manifold activities with respect to guiding ordinary people on the path to enlightenment. Ordinarily the term *karma*, without the particle *pa*, signifies the action of an individual who is overcome by inner bondage.

The first Karmapa, Dusum Khyenpa, established the very first institutionalized reincarnation.[31] Karmapa promised to reincarnate successively in order to lead the new Karmapa Order which he had created. Before dying, in 1193, he gave sealed instructions to a trusted disciple. This prophetic note spelled out the identity of the parents and the location where he was going to be reborn. This procedure has been followed by every reincarnation of the Karmapa, and the instructions have been adhered to scrupulously by the inner circle of faithful disciples, right up to the most recent incarnation of the late Sixteenth

Karmapa, Rangjung Rigpa'i Dorje. The Seventeenth Karmapa was installed recently at the reconstructed Tsurphu monastery near Lhasa.

Since the reincarnation of the first Karmapa, this special system of reincarnate lamas became a dominant feature in the lives of all Tibetan Buddhist orders, and nearly every monastery has one or several reincarnate lamas. The reincarnations of Tibet's spiritual and temporal ruler, the Dalai Lama, began in 1476, when the Second Dalai Lama was discovered, and have continued in an unbroken line right up to the present, the Fourteenth Dalai Lama. Institutional reincarnations, called tulkus in Tibetan, have generally proved to be an especially revitalizing factor in Tibetan Buddhism. Unfortunately, the selection process sometimes gets entangled with petty personal or factional politics. Nonetheless, the reincarnate lamas are highly revered throughout the Tibetan Buddhist world. Recently, some Tibetan lineages have even begun selecting Westerners as the reincarnations of lamas.

There are two kinds of reincarnations, controlled and uncontrolled. "Uncontrolled" refers to sentient beings who have yet to gain control over their lives and destiny. "Controlled" refers to those who have achieved enlightenment, but have chosen to reincarnate at will in another human existence so as to help others who are still afflicted by inner delusions. Such reincarnate individuals—whether recognized or not—are understood to be bodhisattvas.

The reincarnations of the Karmapa have fascinated not only the Tibetans, but Mongolian, Chinese, and Manchu rulers for centuries. The first Karmapa and his successive reincarnations made manifold and lasting contributions toward preserving and spreading Tibetan Buddhism, inspiring the religious quest of Tibetans, and ensuring political stability—through their spiritual powers—in the more volatile and violent regions of China and Mongolia. Some Karmapas, such as the second, third, and fourth, became the personal preceptors to some of the Mongol Khans and Manchu emperors.

Popular reverence of them was strengthened when a number of leading Buddhist teachers, based on specific scriptural prophecies and their own visionary insight, recognized Karmapa as being the reincarnation of the Bodhisattva Avalokiteshvara. The latter is one of the great bodhisattvas, who is seeking to alleviate the miseries of all sentient beings and to guide them toward permanent well-being and enlightenment. Passages in the scriptures of Mahayana Buddhism refer to

Avalokiteshvara's vow before the historical Buddha. In this vow Avalokiteshvara pledged to emerge in diverse emanations so as to serve sentient beings in the "Snowy Land," Tibet. Some specific prophecies revealed that Avalokiteshvara would also emerge as successive monk rulers in the Snowy Land. This was recognized as a specific reference to the successive Dalai Lamas.

The successive Karmapas extended Gampopa's eclectic approach of embracing the teachings of other Tibetan Buddhist orders, notably those of the Nyingmapa School. The various eclectic approaches of particular individuals within the Karmapa order became a dominant movement under the brilliant leadership of Jamgon Kongtrul (1813-1901), the foremost disciple of the Fourteenth Karmapa, who was hailed as an emanation of Manjushri, the bodhisattva of Wisdom. With the collaboration of the renowned *Rime* teacher, Jamyang Khyentse, the great Kongtrul compiled the teachings of esoteric self-realization, which had hitherto been dispersed throughout the various Tibetan Buddhist orders.

The Karmapa Order has been unusually dynamic and successful, except for a temporary period of decline in its prestige during the seventeenth century. Even the violent Chinese takeover of Tibet in 1959 could not stop the Dharma activity of the Karmapa and his followers. Ironically, the exile of this great bodhisattva from Tibet actually contributed toward the worldwide growth of the Karma Kagyu order. In the early 1960's, soon after he had led his community of monks and lay devotees to safety from his monastery in Tibet, the Sixteenth Karmapa established a new monastery, with a separate meditation center, at Rumtek in Sikkim, close to the Tibetan border. He later founded Kagyupa centers in India, Europe, and the U.S.A., and devoted himself to the monumental and invaluable task of publishing beautiful sets of the Tibetan Buddhist scriptures, in 330 volumes, from the original woodblock prints, for distribution to every Tibetan monastery in exile.

Convinced of the vital importance of incarnate teachers, the Sixteenth Karmapa installed reincarnations of many leading incarnate lamas at Rumtek Monastery. Today there are a number of young, energetic incarnate lamas teaching Buddhism, such as the Thirteenth Shamar Tulku (who traces his origin to the first Shamar Dragpa Sengye, 1283-1349), the Twelfth Situ Tulku (who goes back to Situ Chokyi Gyaltsen, 1377-1448), the Twelfth Gyaltsep Tulku (who traces his line of incarnations to the first Goshri Paljor Dondrup, 1427-1489), and the Third Jamgon Kongtrul[32] (whose line goes back to the First Jamgon Kongtrul, 1813-1901).

Although maintaining the traditions and affiliation of the Karma Kagyupa, several local Karma Kagyu branches grew in size, influence, and tradition, to the extent that essentially they became sub-sects. These include the Surmang Kagyupa in the Ga area of east Tibet, and the Naydo Kagyupa in central Tibet.

The Phagdru Kagyupa Order

The Phagdru Kagyupa Order was founded by Gampopa's disciple, Phagdru Dorje Gyalpo (1110-1170), when he built a great monastery in the Tsethang region of south Tibet. Because of his increasing prestige and following, this great teacher was appointed Desi, or chief administrator, of Nedong Province by the Sakyapa ruler of Tibet. This was one of the thirteen myriarchies in the central region of the country.

Dorje Gyalpo made sure that the combined spiritual and political authority remained in the hands of his descendants. One son from every Phagdru family became a monk, so as to hold onto this prestigious position. One of those monks, having suffered much harassment from the Sakya ruler, seized regional and national power in 1354, through a combination of clever strategy and military force. This was Jangchub Gyaltsen (1302-1364), who was honored by the great Kublai Khan with the title of Tai Situ—Great Teacher. He was a wise ruler and was compared to the ancient Tibetan kings. The Phagdru family continued to rule for several generations until they lost power to the head of the Rinpung family during the fifteenth century.

The principle disciples of Phagdru established eight independent orders. They are called the "eight younger orders," namely, the Drikung, Taklung, Trophu, Lingre (or Drukpa), Martsang, Yelpa, Yemsang, and Shugseb.

The Tselpa and Baram Kagyupa Orders

The remaining two of the "four elder schools" of the Kagyupa—the Tselpa and Baram—did not survive independently for a long time. Their unique traditions were absorbed into and continued by the other Kagyupa branches.

The Drikung Kagyupa Order

The Drikungpa are one of the three surviving orders of the original eight younger schools. Their first monastery was established in the Drikung region, on the periphery of the Northern Plateau (Changthang), by the renowned teacher, Kyobpa Jigten Sumgon[33] (1143-1217), one of the chief disciples of Phagdru. The founder belongs to the ranks of Tibet's great teachers by virtue of his scholarship and attainment. His teachings and writings were particularly known for their profundity, clarity, and refreshing approach.

His most important work was the *Drikung Gongchik—The One Thought of Drikung*.[34] This major treatise recasts Buddhism in a fascinating and innovative form, emphasizing each aspect as being capable of revealing the full process of enlightenment. Kyobpa Jigten Sumgon was also revered for his enlightening guidance and humanistic service to the common people. The Drikungpa monastic complex and its branches in eastern Tibet, as well as its sister monasteries in Ladakh (now a region of the Indian Himalayas), are known for their efficient training and groups of cotton-clad "repas," who practice the six branches of the supreme yoga and Mahamudra meditation in high mountain caves.

The Drikung Monastery in Tibet is headed by successive abbots, not always reincarnations. The Drikung order itself is headed by two incarnate lamas: His Holiness Drikung Kyabgon Chetsang Rinpoche and His Holiness Drikung Kyabgon Chungtsang Rinpoche. Chetsang Rinpoche, the thirty-seventh abbot, escaped from Chinese-controlled Tibet to India in 1975; and since then he has been reorganizing the Indian Drikungpa monasteries in Ladakh and Dehra Dun. He has also been actively guiding various Drikung meditation centers in India and the West. The other head, Chungtsang Rinpoche, has remained in Tibet.

The Taklungpa Kagyupa Order

The Taklungpa belong to the aforementioned group of eight younger orders. This school was established by Taklung Thangpa Trashi Pal (1142-1210), one of the principal disciples of Phagmo Drupa in the Taklung[35] area of the Northern Plateau (Changthang). Later, one of its branches was set up in Rewoche, in the Denma region of eastern Tibet, and others were subsequently established in parts of Ü and Tsang (Tibet's central region). The original monastery devoted itself to satisfying the cultural and spiritual needs of pious nomadic tribes.

The Taklung Kagyupa usually concentrate on the original Kagyu teachings, which came from Gampopa. The specific system of Mahamudra they practice is known as the "Mahamudra in Five Aspects" (Chakchen Ngaden). The head of Taklung Monastery is usually a reincarnation of Matrul. In the 1960's, the Taklungpa also re-established a monastic center in India.

The Drukpa Kagyupa Order

The Drukpa Kagyupa is also one of the eight younger orders. There are several loosely connected sub-orders under the common denomination of Drukpa. The first was Lingre Kagyupa, named after the great teacher, Lingchen Repa Pema Dorje (1128-1188). His disciples and their spiritual heirs then established a number of sub-branches. Ling Repa's foremost disciple, Tsangpa Gyare (1161-1211), established Jangchub Ling Monastery in the Nam area of south Tibet. According to the history of the order, a terrifying thunderstorm shook the whole region while the new monastery was being consecrated. The incident was considered a good omen, promising future prosperity and the spread of the Kagyu teachings. Thunder is believed to be the roar of the dragon, *druk* in Tibetan. Thus the term druk was added to the name of the place and the order, and they have since been known as the Drukpa Kagyupa.

After a while, three new branches emerged. They were identified with the geographical locations of their monastic centers: Todruk (the Drukpa Order of the Upper Region), Maydruk (the Drukpa Order of the Lower Region), and Bardruk (the Drukpa Order of the Middle Region).

Further spread of the Drukpa Kagyupa began when a great teacher of the Bardruk branch, Phajo Drukgom Zhikpo, moved to a region further south called Lhomon Khazhi Region (The Four Entrances of Southern Mon). A man of unusual attainment and spiritual power, he successfully established his spiritual dominance over the land and won the submission of other local orders such as the Sakyapa, the Nyingmapa, and the Drikung branch of Lhapa Kagyupa. Before long, the name of the land was changed to Druk Yul, or "Land of the Dragon." To the outside world, it is known as the country of Bhutan.

The turning point in the fate of the Drukpa Kagyupa and that of Drukyul came in the seventeenth century, with the arrival of Zhabdrung Ngawang Namgyal, a high tulku from the first Drukpa Monastery, who was compelled to flee Tibet to escape the persecution of the lay ruler, Dipa Tsangpa at Shigatse. At the time, there were already many Drukpa monasteries in Drukyul. Zhabdrung's spiritual authority was soon acknowledged widely by the inhabitants and the monasteries. He became the first Kagyupa teacher to establish a Buddhist state, with himself as the Dharmaraja—the paramount spiritual sovereign. He and his successive reincarnations ruled Drukyul through regents (Devaraja). This rule by lama was replaced by a hereditary monarchy at the turn of the twentieth century.

In time, the reincarnation of Tsangpa Gyarey, the founder of the original Druk Monastery, moved to a new monastery near the southern border of Tibet. The young reincarnation of Gyalwang Drukchen the Thirteenth heads the monasteries in the eastern Himalayan region of Darjeeling, and also the well-known monastery of Hemis in Ladakh.

The Shangpa Kagyupa Order

The Shangpa Kagyupa Order was established during the early eleventh century, quite independently from the original Kagyupa order founded by Gampopa. The Shangpa Kagyupa were named after the Shang area of Tsang, in the midwestern part of Tibet. The founder was Khyungpo Naljor (987-1079), one of Tibet's greatest scholars, and also a poet, physician, musician, dramatist, humanist, and enlightened teacher. A convert from Tibet's native Bon faith, he studied Buddhism under many teachers in Tibet and India.

While in India, he made a tremendous effort to obtain what was considered a highly secret and rare esoteric doctrine called "The Six Branches of the Buddhist Supreme Yoga," which was practiced by a great woman teacher, the "Awakened Niguma" (who was also the consort of Naropa), and by another woman teacher called Sukha Siddhi. He achieved his aim when he finally met both these women and received the rare teachings he sought. He was even more fortunate when another great esoteric master unexpectedly visited him and gave him a complete self-realization contemplation of the five meditation deities. These two sets of teachings represent the essential doctrines which the Shangpa Kagyupa have preserved and propagated up to the present time.[36]

Khyungpo Naljor was hailed by all Tibetan orders as a pre-eminent scholar and enlightened teacher. He established over one hundred monasteries and trained many thousands of monks.

Mahasiddha Thangtong Gyalpo (1385-1509), who lived to be 124 years old, also hailed from the Shangpa Kagyu Order. A deeply enlightened teacher, Thangtong Gyalpo was revered throughout the entire Tibetan Buddhist world. He was an eminent scholar, poet, physician, musician, and humanist. He is credited with having developed a new way of smelting iron, and used his engineering skills to construct over one hundred iron bridges throughout Tibet.

In our present era, the secret teachings of the Shangpa Kagyupa have been introduced to serious students, both inside and outside of Tibet, by the late Kalu Rinpoche (1905-1989). Kalu Rinpoche was a most accomplished Rime master. He devoted himself fully to giving a variety of esoteric teachings which are usually propagated only by their respective orders.[37] Since Kalu Rinpoche's death in 1989, the Venerable Bokar Rinpoche has succeeded Kalu as head of the Shangpa Kagyu lineage. In February of 1993, the new incarnation of Kalu Rinpoche was enthroned in India at the age of two.

Education

Buddhist education is designed to bring about immediate self-transformation in three ways: scholarship, self-control, and kindness. Students on the advanced level are required to cultivate one important principle: bodhichitta. Bodhichitta means the conscious development of compassionate concern, and a commitment to work for the well-being and enlightenment of all sentient beings. Students are taught how to develop this all-encompassing attitude by practicing the six transcendent virtues (*paramitas*): generosity, morality, tolerance, joyful perseverance, contemplation, and wisdom. The first five represent the skillful means of compassion. The sixth, contemplation on wisdom, is capable of bringing about an all-around calmness, serenity, and sensitivity, while shielding the mind from various inner disturbances such as self-delusion,[38] selfishness, and prejudices.

For an elucidation of the principles and purposes of Buddhist education one may refer to the traditional guidelines called "the three wheels of training": the wheel of study, through listening and examining; the wheel of quiet contemplation, wherein, through the practice of insight meditation or *vipashyana*, one questions what has been taught; and the wheel of benevolent actions, wherein one puts into practice what has been learned and actualized in oneself by guiding and teaching others, and living a life in accord with the Dharma. This educational system, regardless of its constraints, greatly contributed to the refinement of social attitudes and behavior.

The Kagyupas, like other orders, follow the concept and purpose of Buddhist education. Education in a traditional sense is a means for "acquiring essential knowledge and developing authentic qualities." This definition explicitly points to the necessity for thorough learning and high attainment. The Buddhist tradition holds that the mere acquisition of knowledge (other than the technical kind) hinders human development and unleashes certain (often degenerative) impulses which the egoistic attitudes produce. Buddhist education is designed to foster in every individual an all-round development, so that a person can help others advance their permanent well-being.

Buddhist education is confined primarily to monasteries, nunneries, and tutorial residences in Tibet. The Kagyupa monasteries, like those of other orders, are organized to perform various functions. The main function is to preserve the Buddhist teachings and traditions and to serve ordinary people by fulfilling their educational, cultural, and religious needs. The many levels of Buddhist studies are designed to meet the different needs of students. There is no uniformity in the educational syllabus. For instance, the Sakyapas and Gelugpas consider Shedra, the school of Buddhist dialectics, essential for a student's thorough grounding in Buddhist doctrine, whereas the Nyingmapa and Kagyupa orders consider it complimentary to meditation.

The subjects studied consist of the five essential ones: Vinaya (moral and monastic laws), Abhidharma (the theory of mental and material realities), Pramana (logic and epistemology), Madhyamika (the central philosophy), and Prajnaparamita (transcendent wisdom). The Kagyupa schools of dialectics study these five subjects through thirteen major treatises, and some have enlarged this to eighteen, plus the commentaries. Only some select monasteries of the Karmapa and Drikungpa orders have introduced the educational medium of dialectics and group debates, apparently having adopted these from the Gelugpa and the preceding Kadampa orders.

Most Kagyupa monasteries do not have dialectically oriented studies, but rather continue with a simpler system which relies on close contact between teacher and students. The teacher explains a given text in a number of ways. Then, gradually, the older students assume the role of explaining it, under the supervision of the teacher. This was the original method of Kagyupa studies from the time of Marpa, Milarepa, and Gampopa.

To provide a special, intensive training in the meditation systems, there were meditation centers called Drubdra. Kagyupas consider meditation to be of vital importance in an individual's training. These centers start by providing condensed comprehensive courses in Buddhism, using, for instance, Gampopa's *Jewel Ornament of Liberation* as the basic text. Monastic students who have completed the major studies at schools of dialectics, or the general course at non-dialectic monasteries, then join a meditation center. There they receive from the abbot or principal lama instructions on a series of preparatory exercises, ranging from physical prostration to vocal recitation, contemplative visualization, rapid comprehension, and averting obstacles. Meditators engage in these exercises by completing each part one hundred thousand times.

Once this is done, and if the lama is pleased, he grants one or more major empowerments, leading to the intensive meditation retreat. The most cherished and practiced teaching in most Kagyupa monastic centers is the contemplation on the meditation deity, Chakrasamvara—The All-Accomplishing Wheel. The advanced study of esoteric tantra is not limited to this alone. Monks study a variety of esoteric systems, selected from the vast body of tantric scriptures, under a variety of lamas.

Having studied the theory and practice of a given system of self-realization, including the relevant secret oral instructions, a student undertakes a thirty-nine month intensive meditation retreat alone, or with a group of initiates, in some hermitage or mountain retreat. Often, serious practitioners repeat this intensive course, or even become lifelong meditators.

The education of senior monks is far more extensive than that of ordinary students, so that many of them can assume the responsibility of abbots, instructors, and teachers. Even though incarnate lamas (tulkus) are treated as predestined teachers (lamas), they must earn the institutional honor by competing with learned monks in group debate before the entire assembly, or by passing a direct tutorial assignment. Besides participating in courses, incarnate lamas, especially the heads of an order, study with a full-time residential tutor (yongdzin). As they reach an advanced level, they go to as many great teachers as they wish and receive a variety of teachings, including the secret oral transmissions.

Under any monastic order there is a set of subjects which may be studied, wholly or partly, formally or privately, in the full course of Buddhist studies. Among these are Sanskrit, medicine, astronomy, astrology, and sacred arts and crafts.

All these studies are done through the medium of classical Tibetan. Like Buddhism, the classical Tibetan language has always been a unifying factor in Tibet. Through a distinctive method of study, all monastic students are required to memorize numerous texts representing sets of liturgies, outlines of major subjects, and ritualistic and meditation materials. They are also required to master the different forms of liturgical chanting and choral office; but only select groups are trained in special ritual music, the art of sand mandala, painting of sacred scrolls (thangkas), sculpting of butter sculptures for symbolic offerings, and so forth. In addition, each monastery (as a self-contained institution) trains monks, nuns, and lay people in a variety of administrative positions, such as managers, secretaries, stewards, scribes, traders, and so on.

Last but not least, there is the Buddhist education of lay people. Aside from charitable schools, which provided basic literary skills and religious education, there were established ways of pursuing both general and specialized Buddhist studies. Serious lay people could follow desired courses under one or several chosen teachers, and also participate in public discourses sponsored by generous patrons. Such courses were open to anyone interested. Well-to-do families often invited highly revered teachers to live at their residence.

Monasteries usually opened their doors to lay people and encouraged direct contact. They received pilgrims year-round and provided religious services at homes of ordinary people. Many monasteries invited the public to their festivals and sacred dances. Monk physicians visited villages to treat the sick, infirm, and aged. Monastic centers were not only repositories of sacred artifacts but continuing sources of new production, always acting as patrons of artists producing sacred art. Lay devotees did the same by acquiring religious art for their private shrines. There was—and still is—significant mutual contact between the religious and secular communities, which accounts in no small way for the harmony in Tibetan communities. Lay devotees received the gift of Dharma from the religious community, and, in exchange, reverentially provided material support to the monasteries.

There are far more similarities than differences between the Kagyupas and other orders. Only some of the distinguishing features are outlined here. From their inception, the Kagyupas consisted of many different groups. Yet their lack of homogeneity actually enhanced the individual dynamism each order had demonstrated. In some Kagyupa monasteries one sees a rather uncommon sight of a mixed congregation, consisting of red-robed, clean-shaven monks, and white-robed yogins (realized ones), wearing heavy hair tufted upward and a pair of round ivory earrings.

Many great Kagyupa teachers showed an independence of spirit and power of vision throughout their life and ministry. This was evident in the establishment of the various monastic orders and also in the reformulating of Buddhist doctrines and the interpretation of the concept of reality, as well as the practice of meditation. Some even advanced radical views which evoked widespread criticism. One can observe a diversity of opinion among great teachers with regard to their doctrinal views of ultimate reality.

The Kagyupa system of Mahamudra (the quintessence of mind and meditation) reveals a special approach and insight. Regardless of the nonconformist tendencies of some eminent teachers, the Kagyupas in general have followed Gampopa's teachings faithfully.

The most cherished gifts that the original Kagyupa masters brought from India to Tibet were the tantras, represented by and embodied in the symbolic figures of such meditation deities as Chakrasamvara and Vajravarahi, to mention just a couple. The doctrine and practices associated with these two deities are revealed in the Supreme Yoga class of tantra (Anuttara-tantra). The name Chakrasamvara, literally translated, means "The Wheel that Encompasses Everything," meaning that the supreme wisdom embraces all cosmic phenomena. Here, and in general, a male figure represents compassion, while a female represents wisdom.

All Vajrayana deities belong to the five Buddha families and their feminine consorts, the five wisdom dakinis. Each Buddha family symbolizes an essential state of the buddha-mind (dharmakaya). The appearance, color, hands, gesture, position, and implements convey manifold messages, including coded ones for initiates.

Specifically, the figure of Chakrasamvara symbolizes the supreme illusory form, signifying that all appearances are merely illusion, devoid of any intrinsic essence. His dark blue color symbolizes the all-encompassing void (sarva-shunyata) immanent in all realities. His three eyes indicate complete knowledge of the three periods of time.[39] His four faces symbolize compassion, kindness, joy, and equanimity (the four immeasurables). His twelve arms symbolize the twelve links of interdependent co-arising[40] relating to the transitory events of existence. The jewel necklace on his head symbolizes the two inseparable principles of compassion and wisdom.

Vajravarahi, the consort of Chakrasamvara, is the embodiment of supreme wisdom. Her red color symbolizes great bliss; her nudity represents the elimination of all inner defilements. In short, the male and female figures in intimate sexual embrace represent the unity of apparent reality and its ultimate voidness, and also the inseparability of compassion and wisdom.

The Chakrasamvara self-realization system is the heart of the Kagyupa religious tradition. This practice, centered around the meditation deity, consists of the two main stages (the visualized contemplation and the consummate meditation),[41] as well as the six branches of the Buddhist supreme yoga. There are two versions of the six yogas, one of which came from Naropa and the other from his consort Niguma.[42]

The Kagyupa Order thus plays a significant role in preserving the teachings of Buddhism, seeking to advance the enduring well-being and enlightenment of all sentient beings. The Kagyupa orders show their dedication in their contemplative system. They regard meditation as the only reliable and effective means of achieving an authentic insight into the ultimate nature of mind and reality, and for developing noble qualities.

In general, the Kagyupas conclude that the rational determination of the ultimate can produce only a definite intellectual comprehension, but it is incapable of bringing about an authentic insight. Milarepa's criticism of the rational approach that is routinely applied by dialecticians is the best example of this attitude.[43]

This essay is intended to show the vital role that Kagyupas have played, since the eleventh century, in preserving and promoting in Tibet the complete Buddhist doctrines and practices which are collectively known as the three vehicles of Buddha Dharma.

From the time of Marpa, Milarepa, and Gampopa, Tibet began to transform into a vibrant sacred realm (chodan zhinkham). The Tibetan landscape was marked with colorful temples, monasteries, stupas, and prayer flags. Equally commendable are the invaluable contributions— moral and material—made by Tibetans in every walk of life. The Tibetans were truly a peaceful people living in resplendent isolation.

However, Tibet was invaded and occupied by Mao's Red Army in 1950. China's ruthless destruction and suppression of Tibet and its people began with full fury in 1959. The Tibetans are still treated with contempt and cruelty in their own country. Tibet as we know it is being virtually eliminated. Tibetan refugees living in exile, with renewed determination, devote themselves to the preservation of the Tibetan community, culture, and—above all—the precious teachings of Buddhism, under the wise and compassionate leadership of His Holiness the Fourteenth Dalai Lama.

Virtually every family considered it their sacred duty to send at least one son to a monastery. During the past nine centuries of recorded Tibetan history the Kagyupa monasteries and teachers have made a lasting and visible contribution to the religious education and culture of the Tibetan people. Since 1959, when many thousands of Tibetan people fled the occupation armies of the Communist Chinese and scattered about the globe, the treasures of the Kagyu lineage, preserved intact from Gampopa to the present, are now bringing well-being and wisdom to people of all races and countries.

The Mahamudra: Gampopa's System of Tibetan Buddhist Meditation

by Jampa Mackenzie Stewart

Gampopa played a significant role in the synthesis, refinement and development of the various meditative traditions of Tibet. Now, nearly 1,000 years after his death, the influence of his genius pervades the training of Tibetan Buddhist monks and lay people.

Gampopa was a master and lineage holder of two distinctly different Buddhist meditation systems. The first of these was the monastic Kadampa system, brought to Tibet in the mid-eleventh century by the Indian monk Atisha. The second was the yogic system of the Indian Buddhist mahasiddhas, introduced into Tibet by Marpa the Translator, and transmitted to Gampopa through Milarepa. Gampopa used his vast knowledge and experience to combine and synthesize these two approaches into a new system, which he called the Mahamudra. His new lineage subsequently became known as the Dakpo Kagyupa.

The Kadampa system, which formed the foundation of Gampopa's training, integrated the entire spectrum of Buddhist teachings into a systematic and progressive approach to spiritual development. Central to Atisha's presentation of the Dharma was the Lam Rim, or The Graduated Path To Enlightenment.

The Lam Rim system emphasizes the importance of a thorough grounding in the Hinayana and Mahayana scriptures and practices as a firm foundation for the higher level tantric and Mahamudra practices. The Lam Rim teachings recognize that spiritual aspirants enter the path with relatively different capacities, scopes, and levels of aspiration. It gently guides the aspirant from the initial motivation—seeking liberation for oneself from the dissatisfaction and suffering of samsara—through to the attainment of complete Buddhahood, with the aspiration of working to bring all living beings to the same goal.

The Lam Rim method of meditative training begins with an assessment of our human condition. Life is impermanent, without anything that is solid and lasting to cling to for happiness and stability. Eventually death claims everyone, and we can take no family, friends, or possessions with us to the grave. The only things that we do take with us are the seeds of karma, our good or evil actions of thought, word, and deed, which will bear fruit in subsequent lifetimes. Therefore, it is important to take responsibility for ourselves, to abandon negative actions and to practice positive actions ceaselessly throughout our lives. This aspiration, to practice morality in order to be reborn into a higher level birth as a human or god, is known as the "small aspiration."

Nonetheless, even if we practice positive actions and are reborn into a human or god realm existence, these pleasant situations are not lasting. We are still within samsara and we will still find suffering. We must give up all attachment to samsara and cultivate ourselves spiritually if we wish to be free from the cycle of endless death and rebirth.

It is within the human form that spiritual cultivation is most effective; if we have the opportunity and leisure for spiritual development in this lifetime, we must treat this human birth as a precious opportunity and not waste it. The path at this level of practice is to make an honest assessment of our situation through analytical contemplation of the aforementioned points. Through this analysis, the practitioner forms a firm resolve to renounce samsara. He or she also takes vows to practice moral conduct, to avoid negative actions, and to practice positive actions. In addition, one takes refuge in the Three Jewels: The Buddha, the Dharma, and the Sangha, and makes a commitment to rely on them as trustworthy guides on the path to peace.

The meditation training at this level includes the contemplative or analytical meditations on impermanence and death, the precious human birth, karma, and the sufferings of samsara. These are known as the "four thoughts that turn the mind to religion." They are also known as the Four Ordinary Foundations, or ngondro—the preliminary practices.

In addition, the aspirant is taught morality, meditation, and mindfulness. The two basic levels of meditation are shamatha or tranquil abiding meditation, and vipashyana or insight meditation. Tranquil abiding meditation is divided into nine stages of calming the mind and bringing it to a state of clear, lucid, and concentrated focus.[44] Once the mind can be imperturbably concentrated, one can practice the analytical meditations of insight meditation for developing penetrating awareness into the nature of mind and reality.[45]

Having accomplished these, one then goes deeper into the eight stages of samadhi or meditative absorption, and begins to cultivate the view of emptiness or *shunyata*.[46] The result is the attainment of arhatship, or the slightly higher level of a pratyekabuddha. This motivation is known as the "middling level of aspiration." These attainments are considered lower levels of realization; they bring individual liberation from suffering, but they do not bring one to full Buddhahood.[47] This is the Hinayana level of training.

Those of greater capacity go on to cultivate the altruistic motivation—bodhichitta—the desire to attain enlightenment in order to be able to lead all beings in the universe to liberation. They cannot bear the thought of leaving cyclic existence merely to achieve peace for themselves, while other beings are still caught in the web of confusion and suffering. Aspirants at this stage take the Bodhisattva Vow, committing themselves to cultivating both relative and absolute bodhichitta.

Relative bodhichitta is divided into two types: aspiration bodhichitta, wherein one cultivates the motivation to help others at all times, and practical bodhichitta, wherein one actually practices the *six paramitas* to benefit beings. Both the relative and absolute stages of bodhichitta are subsumed under the cultivation of the six paramitas. The first five paramitas—generosity, patience, ethics, enthusiastic diligence, and meditative concentration—are seen as the actions of relative bodhichitta, as they are still taking place within a dualistic perspective; one still thinks and acts in terms of self and other, and within this relative framework one is benefiting others. Development of these five paramitas is known as the accumulation of merit.

The sixth paramita—wisdom or *prajna* paramita—develops the wisdom that cognizes emptiness, the absolute non-dual mind of awakening. Development of prajna paramita is known as the accumulation of wisdom. The practice of the six paramitas is not necessarily linear and progressive; wisdom and merit are usually developed side by side. The various levels of Bodhisattva realization—the stages of awakening on the way to complete Buddhahood—are measured in terms of understanding and mastering the various paramitas. This is the essence of the Mahayana path.

Once one is firmly established in the Mahayana, one can begin to employ the many skillful methods of the *Tantrayana*. In Gampopa's tradition, the tantric path begins with the extraordinary level of ngondro, or foundation practice.

Ngondro consists of four basic practices. The first is refuge and bodhichitta, wherein one recites the prayers of refuge and performs full length prostrations before a visualized image of one's own guru, surrounded by all the sources of refuge. This practice strengthens one's faith and commitment to the tantric path, and removes obstacles to accomplishment.

The second is the Vajrasattva meditation. Here one visualizes Vajrasattva, the primordial Buddha whose one hundred-syllable mantra one recites for purification. In this practice, one confesses one's negative karma, illnesses, and sins. Then one receives healing and purifying nectar-light from Vajrasattva, and visualizes that all one's sins are forgiven, washed away, and that all one's illnesses are healed. In this purified state, one visualizes that Vajrasattva dissolves into oneself, and imagines that one has actually been transformed into Vajrasattva Buddha. By visualizing oneself in the form of a Buddha, reciting mantra, and meditating on the emptiness of all appearances, one purifies, respectively, the karmic tendencies of one's body, speech, and mind, and plants the karmic seeds for the attainment of the transcendent body, speech, and mind of a Buddha.

The third practice of ngondro is the mandala offering. Here one imagines that the entire universe, with all of its wealth, belongs to oneself. One then makes a mandala offering representing the entire universe to the refuge sources, in gratitude for their gift of the Dharma. In this way one cultivates a sense of non-attachment to material appearances, a sense of generosity, and accumulates great merit, or virtuous karma, that will help one to realize the auspicious karmic conditions necessary for the realization of Buddhahood.

The fourth practice of ngondro is guru yoga. Here one visualizes one's guru in front of oneself in the form of a Buddha. One prays to one's guru, visualizes that wisdom light radiates from the guru's four chakras into one's own chakras, granting blessings and empowerments, removing obstacles, and planting the seeds for realization. Then the guru dissolves into light and merges with oneself. By seeing one's guru as a fully awakened Buddha, developing great devotion, and by visualizing one's guru merging inseparably with oneself, one can begin to awaken one's own dormant Buddha potential.[48]

Generally one is said to have completed the ngondro when one has completed one hundred thousand repetitions of each practice. However, it is not the number of recitations completed, but the quality of one's attainment that is the goal of ngondro. In addition, even after having completed them, the ngondro practices are still incorporated into Highest Yoga Tantra sadhanas as a preliminary preparation.

Upon completing ngondro, one will have acquired skill at visualization, and will have become familiar with basic meditations on emptiness. At this stage, one proceeds on to a more profound level of guru yoga, practicing the outer, inner, and secret levels of guru yoga. All the Kagyu lineages include the guru yogas of Marpa, Milarepa, and Gampopa; the various Kagyupa branches also incorporate the guru yogas of their specific lineage founders, such as the guru yoga of Karmapa in the Karma Kagyu lineage and Lord Jigten Sumgon in the Drikung Kagyu.

Thus, guru yoga is both a preliminary practice and a main practice in the path of Mahamudra. All the great masters have emphasized that when one forms a pure bond with one's guru, engenders uncontrived devotion toward the guru, and practices according to the guru's instructions, then one receives the river of blessings flowing from the lineage, and Mahamudra realization follows swiftly and naturally with few obstacles. However, without true devotion to the qualified guru, realization is next to impossible. Saraha states in his *Queen Doha*:

> Only a holy guru can bring about the understanding
> That in emptiness all diverse phenomena
> Are one and the same.
> This supremely noble one is like the water unto swans.
> Pay your homage to him with deep veneration![49]

The subsequent stages of tantra focus on deity yoga: visualizing oneself in transcendent form, wherein each aspect of one's appearance is symbolic of an aspect of awakened mind. Favorite tantric deities of the Kagyupa lineage of Gampopa are Vajrayogini, Chakrasamvara, and Hevajra.

Thus, through the practice of Vajrayana one gradually develops a firm sense of commitment, purifies obstacles, accumulates tremendous merit, inspires great uncontrived devotion, and loosens the hold of habitual negative patterns, to allow space for the dawning of wisdom. This prepares one to receive the teachings and transmission of blessings from the lineage gurus: one's body, speech and mind become fertile ground for the ultimate realization of the true nature of mind, or Mahamudra.

Using practices such as deity yoga and visualization, mantra, mudras, symbols, breathing exercises, and ritual, can geometrically accelerate one's progress to Buddhahood. For this reason tantra is often called "the short path." Like a short cut up a mountain, one can reach the peak more quickly and directly, but it is usually steeper and more dangerous. Without a firm foundation, it is easy for misunderstandings and abuse of the teachings to occur.[50] This was in fact what had happened in Tibet before Atisha arrived, and for this reason Atisha only revealed the tantric teachings to his closest disciples.[51] He also emphasized monasticism as the foundation for Dharma teaching and practice.

Gampopa already had a thorough grounding in the Kadampa practices of the Hinayana, Mahayana, and the lower levels of tantric practice at the time he left the monastery to study with the reclusive mountain yogi, Milarepa. The mahasiddha tradition of Milarepa was a strong tantric tradition, more condensed and quintessential than that of the Kadampas. Although it included the essence of the Hinayana and Mahayana within each yogic meditation session, there was little emphasis on scholastic study of the Hinayana and Mahayana sutras. Instead there was heavy emphasis on direct insight into the true nature of mind through meditative practice, and on the actual transformation of one's ordinary body, speech, and mind into the transcendent body, speech, and mind of a Buddha, through the completion stage yogas of the method path.

Many yogic practices that work with the prana or inner energy in the body, notably the Six Yogas of Naropa, were used by the mahasiddhas as a form of internal spiritual alchemy to speed up the transformative processes of Mahamudra realization. These practices break down the calcified layers of ignorance on their energetic level, and thus transform the root neurological patterns of ignorance into wisdom patterns—dawning of the true nature of mind—giving rise to wisdom not just as intellectual understanding, but as direct and conscious experience.

The ultimate fruit of their practice, as well as the path, is the realization of Mahamudra, a word virtually synonymous with Buddhahood. It means the "Great Seal" or "Sublime Stance," the spontaneous embodiment of the all-knowing wisdom and limitless compassion of a Buddha. It is described as "...the attainment of the ultimate mystical experience of the oneness of all things, the non-dual cognition of ultimate reality, clear light, gnostic awareness—the dissolution of the individuated personality in the universal mind. The Buddha's enlightenment is specifically defined as coincident with a vast, empathetic, self-sacrificial, social sensibility—love, in fact."[52]

The stages of development in highest Mahamudra practice are often presented as "the four yogas of Mahamudra." Each of these four are subdivided into three levels: lesser, average, and great attainment. In this way, the four yogas are sometimes referred to as the "twelve stages of Mahamudra."

The first is the "yoga of one-pointedness," wherein one perfects the Mahamudra level of shamatha or tranquil abiding meditation. Unlike the Hinayana tranquil abiding practice, where one applies antidotes to "mental defilements" as they arise, or the ordinary Mahayana methods, wherein one seeks to give up attachment to all mind forms, in Mahamudra tranquil abiding one cultivates a calm and undistracted mind by maintaining the object of meditation while neither suppressing nor encouraging thoughts. Instead one calmly observes the ground from which thoughts appear to arise, where they exist, and to where they disappear, and eventually one perceives that thoughts are merely the radiance of the dharmakaya mind.

Without the ability to imperturbably focus the mind, any subsequent insights will be fleeting. Gampopa gives the following advice at this stage:

> Let your mind remain like the sky without clouds!
> Let your mind remain like an ocean without waves!
> Let your mind remain like a butter lamp without a breeze![53]

The signs of attainment are bliss, clarity, and non-conceptuality. However, the student is admonished not to become attached to these meditative experiences nor to mistake these experiences for ultimate realization; they are like the first signs of light in the morning before the sun has risen.

Next is the "yoga of simplicity," wherein one begins the Mahamudra level of vipashyana or insight meditation. At this stage, clinging to self is completely uprooted, and one perceives the emptiness of both subject and object. All that arises is seen in its pure and unfabricated state; one realizes the unborn and undying nondual nature of phenomena, and one directly perceives the lack of inherent existence in anything. With these realizations one accomplishes the first through the seventh bodhisattva stages.

Next is the "yoga of one taste." In this yoga the practitioner realizes that there is no separation between outer phenomena and mind. This experience of the intrinsic inseparability and oneness of all diverse appearances leads to the total dissolution of acceptance and rejection; one sees all thoughts as the dharmakaya, and that samsara and nirvana are inseparable. All of the kleshas and gross obscurations of habitual mental clinging are irrevocably cleared away, but the subtle obscurations to wisdom still remain. Accomplishment of the yoga of one taste is equivalent to the eighth through the tenth bodhisattva stages.

Ultimately, Mahamudra is the unceasing experience of the true nature of mind without artifice. Even the subtle obscurations are cleared away, and one reaches complete enlightenment of Buddhahood. This final stage of realization is the "yoga of no more meditation," where one remains in the state of Mahamudra awareness with no formal practice. Attempts to do practice at the higher levels actually become impediments to realization. Thus Milarepa instructed Gampopa in his song of farewell:

> When you practice Mahamudra
> Do not busy yourself in practicing your daily rituals
> Of virtuous deeds with body and speech,
> Lest the wisdom of non-distinction vanishes.
> Son, rest in the unfabricated innate nature of mind.
> Do you understand this, monk from U?

Gampopa summarizes the four yogas as follows:

> A lucid, unceasing, momentary awareness
> Is the one-pointed stage of yoga.

> Understanding the essential state of that awareness
> As non-arising [emptiness,]
> Which transcends conceptual modes of reality and unreality,
> Is the non-discriminatory yoga [of simplicity.]

> Understanding diverse appearances as being one
> From the standpoint of their intrinsic nature,
> Is the one-flavor yoga.

> An unceasing realization of the union
> Of appearance and its intrinsic emptiness
> Is the great equipoise of the non-meditation yoga.[54]

This is fruition Mahamudra. One realizes that the true nature of mind is the dharmakaya, emptiness; the radiance of the mind is the sambhogakaya, luminosity; and its manifest form activity is the nirmanakaya, unobstructed compassion.

Highest Mahamudra teachings were not ordinarily given until the student had received tantric *initiation* and had also demonstrated considerable progress along the Tantrayana path. Gampopa broke new ground by bestowing Mahamudra teachings on many, but not all, of his disciples without first giving them any tantric empowerment. Gampopa's scriptural basis for this action was the *Uttaratantra-shastra* by Maitreya-Asanga, a pivotal text in bridging the sutras and tantras. Go Lotsawa said that Gampopa was able to produce an understanding of Mahamudra in these disciples even without initiation. Although Gampopa was criticized by many teachers for instructing in this way, others saw it as an act of compassion in making the Mahamudra teachings available to those who could not receive or maintain the teachings, methods, and commitments of higher tantra.[55]

Since Gampopa's time, many monks, yogis, and lay students have practiced the path of Mahamudra as synthesized by Gampopa, and have achieved the heights of spiritual realization as a result. Gampopa's own enlightenment is evident not only through his many written works, which illustrate an extraordinary depth of scholasticism and understanding, but also through the vigor of his prolific spiritual lineage, still carrying the light of his wisdom and compassion to people of all races around the world.

Notes

1. The banner of victory is one of the eight auspicious symbols. This special name for Milarepa, Mila Dorje Gyaltsen in Tibetan, was revealed to his guru, Marpa, the night before Milarepa's arrival. Milarepa says in *The Life of Milarepa,* p. 43:

> The night before my arrival at Drowo Lung, Marpa saw the Great Master Naropa in a dream. The latter blessed him. He gave him a slightly tarnished, five-pronged vajra (scepter) made of lapis lazuli. At the same time he gave him a golden vase filled with nectar and told him, 'With the water in this vase wash the dirt from the vajra, then mount it on top of the banner of victory. This will please the Buddhas of the past and make all sentient beings happy, thus fulfilling both your aim and that of others.'
>
> Then Naropa vanished. Following the instructions of his Master, Marpa washed the vajra with water from the vase, and mounted it on top of the banner of victory. Then the brilliance of this vajra lit up the whole universe. Immediately the six classes of beings, struck with wonder by its light, were freed from sorrow and filled with happiness. They prostrated themselves and paid reverence to the Venerable Marpa and his banner of victory, which had been consecrated by the Buddhas of the past.

2. The vulture is often referred to as "the high flyer," the one who soars to the heights, symbolizing Milarepa's persistent journey to the highest levels of realization.

3. Geshe Chennawa was a direct disciple of Dromtonpa. This admonition was to play an important role in Gampopa's assimilation of Milarepa's teachings. See Jampa Thaye, *A Garland of Gold: The Early Kagyu Masters in India and Tibet,* p. 53-55.

4. There are several layers of meaning here. One is the sense as conveyed in the story, that Milarepa had been psychically aware of Gampopa throughout his journey and had sent various manifestations of himself to aid Gampopa when needed.

There is an inner meaning as well. In the central tantric meditation practice of guru yoga, one uses the skillful means of seeing one's own guru as the Buddha. One then meditates until one realizes that the guru's mind and one's own mind are inseparable, and have in fact never been separated since beginningless time. In this way one awakens to one's own Buddha mind.

5. In *The One Hundred Thousand Songs of Milarepa*, Mila's "special blessing" was urinating into the pot!

6. Tantra is divided into four classes: Kriya, Carya, Yoga, and Anuttara-yoga. The Mahamudra teachings and the completion stage yogas that work with the channels, winds, and drops are not taught in the lower levels of tantra, but are only found at the quintessential level of Anuttara-yoga Tantra (Highest Yoga Tantra).

7. It is said that Atisha's training for his disciples was founded on a graded path to perfecting bodhichitta, and upon gradually deepening the understanding of the Mahayana view of emptiness, as set forth by Nagarjuna and Chandrakirti. It is often stated by both Nyingmapa and Sarmapa masters that one must establish a theoretical and conceptual understanding of emptiness as a foundation for guiding one's mind to a direct perception of the true nature of mind. I interpret Milarepa's meaning here to be that the emphasis in Atisha's Kadampa training at the tantric level did not go beyond establishing an intellectual understanding of the practice.

8. See Khenpo Könchog Gyaltsen, *The Great Kagyu Masters*, pp. 190-191.

Garma C.C. Chang also writes in his foreword to *Teachings of Tibetan Yoga*, pp. 12-14:

> ...An important theory, underlying the practice of Tibetan Yogas, called 'The Identity of Prana and Mind,' should also be mentioned here. Tantrism views the world as consisting of contrasting, antithetical elements and relationships: noumenon and phenomenon, potentiality and manifestation, reason and affect, Nirvana and Samsara...Prana and Mind. Each of the dualities, though apparently antithetical, is, in reality, an inseparable unity. If one can understand completely and master one member of the duality, he automatically understands and masters the other. Thus, he who realizes the essence of mind as being Transcendental Wisdom will at the same time realize the essence of prana as being inexhaustible vitality and the act of Buddhahood....One of the more important [aspects of this doctrine is] 'the reciprocal character of mind and prana.' This means that a certain type of mind, or mental activity, is invariably accompanied by a prana of corresponding character, whether transcendental or mundane [jnanaprana or karmaprana]....
> Basing itself upon this principle, Tibetan Tantrism offers two Paths,

or types of Yoga, both leading to the same supramundane goal. One is called the Path of Liberation, or 'Mind Yoga,' and the other the Path of Skillfulness (method) or 'Energy Yoga.'

By directing the prana through the wisdom channels of the body through the inner heat yoga and other yogas of the Six Yogas of Naropa, one can invoke a direct experience of the related transcendent wisdom.

9. Gyaltsen, *Kagyu Masters*, p. 190:

It is not enough to gain an intellectual understanding of highest yoga tantra; your mind must absorb and become united with its actual intended meaning. Thus the instructions you receive must have been handed down through an unbroken succession of masters that can be traced back through your present spiritual mentor to Buddha Vajradhara himself. It is absolutely essential that you receive the appropriate empowerments as well as the verbal instructions from such a fully qualified vajra master.

In Vajrayana, the guru, as one of the three roots of refuge, is considered the source of all blessings. By opening completely to the guru with uncontrived devotion, the disciple can receive immeasurable blessings from both the guru and the lineage masters.

10. The fault here is that one falls into the extreme view of nihilism, fails to recognize the relative appearances of cause and effect, and cultivates a grasping mind that holds non-existence as an object.

11. One should see that the very nature of mental defilements and conflicting emotions is not separate from emptiness, so there is nothing to purify. Otherwise one makes the mistake of seeing both the thoughts and emotions as real, and emptiness as something separate, to be applied as an antidote.

12. Although Mahamudra is often discussed in terms of ground Mahamudra, path Mahamudra, and fruition Mahamudra, these are conveniences for the sake of clarity. In essence, the ground, path, and fruit are one. For further discussion of these points, see Takpo Tashi Namgyal, *Mahamudra: the Quintessence of Mind and Meditation*, pp. 293-299; and the Ninth Karmapa Wangchug Dorje, *Mahamudra: Eliminating the Darkness of Ignorance*, translated and edited by Alexander Berzin, pp. 121-125.

13. The method path deals primarily with gaining control of the bodily channels or nadis, energy-winds or pranas, and drops or bindus. The pranas are classified into two general categories: karmaprana, or the karmic energies stemming from ignorance that make us crave rebirth in the samsaric realms; and jnanaprana, or wisdom prana, the purified energies of enlightened consciousness. Each of these two categories of prana is subdivided into five subcategories relating to the five elements.

See Kelsang Gyatso, *Clear Light of Bliss*, p. 25.

14. Tibetan yogic texts say that each person is created from the union of the red drop (representing the menstrual blood) of the mother, and the white

drop (semen) of the father. Once we are conceived and born, the white drop rises to the brain and the red drop descends to the navel center. See Kalsang Gyatso, *Clear Light of Bliss*.

15. Through training in both illusory body yoga and dream yoga, one can actually manifest the illusory body in one's dream body. In this way one thoroughly understands the nature of dreams.

16. This refers to the superiority of the skillful means of the Vajrayana over the Hinayana and the Mahayana sutra teachings.

17. The inner virtues are mastery of meditation, and realization of emptiness and compassion. His outer virtues were his pure samaya in keeping the vows of the three vehicles, and his knowledge and mastery of the various traditions.

18. One of the ways of cultivating compassion used in Mahayana Buddhism is to reflect upon the kindness and self-sacrifice of one's parents, and of one's mother in particular. Then one contemplates that from beginningless time until now, all beings in the universe have, at one time or another, been our mother in the cycle of death and rebirth. Considering that all beings have once shown us such nurturing kindness, and that they are now caught in the net of samsaric suffering, one resolves to repay their kindness by attaining Buddhahood oneself, and then leading all beings out of confused existence.

19. According to Khenpo Karthar Rinpoche, this symbolized that Gampopa would never again experience hindrances in his sleep or dream state, and that he would be able to transform his sleeping state into luminous clear light, the highest attainment of dream yoga. See also Namkhai Norbu, *Dream Yoga and the Practice of Natural Light*.

20. This is because the path of the practitioner at the Hinayana level is different from the path of the tantrika. The Hinayana path is known as the path of renunciation, while the tantric path is the path of transformation. A Hinayana practitioner will thus shun poison, while a tantrika will transform it into nourishing nectar. Thus it would be confusing and detrimental to a tantrika to spend too much time in close company with those on the Hinayana level.

21. Approximately June.

22. The year of the Wood Rabbit, 1135 C.E.

23. The time and places of Gampopa's years of solitary retreat vary according to the different accounts. *A Garland of Gold* states that after leaving Milarepa, Gampopa meditated for three years at Sewalung in Nyel, at the end of which he realized the true nature of mind. He then moved to Ode Kungyal where he lived in solitary retreat for another nine years. At the conclusion of this time, he remembered his guru's parting words and began to journey toward Chuwar, where he met Rechungpa and heard the sad news of Milarepa's passing.

24. Gampopa is said to have accomplished full enlightenment at this time, while maintaining the pure monastic vows of celibacy. It is said by some that

in Highest Yoga Tantra, to attain the final stage of Buddhahood, one must either take a yogic sexual consort (karmamudra) or wait until the moment of death to complete the ultimate realization of Buddhahood. Nonetheless, the Kagyu lamas claim that Gampopa accomplished Buddhahood without relying on a consort nor waiting for death.

We must also remember that most accounts credit Shakyamuni Buddha with attaining ultimate realization during his lifetime without relying on a consort. Still, there are some tantric scholars who assert that Shakyamuni took Sujata, the cowherd maiden who saved his life in the forest, as his consort before his great realization. Also, the *Guhyasamaja Tantra* asserts that to achieve his final realization, the Buddha entered into the samadhi know as "Vajra Glory Partaking of All Desires," and made love with the dakinis of the four directions and the center simultaneously. As he fulfilled the desires of each of the dakinis, they brought him to completion.

It is interesting to note that the accounts observe that Gampopa's patroness was not only wealthy but beautiful as well. She is described as a "female incarnation," which could be a veiled way of describing her as a dakini. Still, the story is not explicit, leaving these points to speculation.

25. Khetsun Sangpo Rinpoche, in *Tantric Practice in Nyingma*, p. 187, comments:

> There are two modes of practice: the sudden and the gradual. The sudden mode is for someone who over many lifetimes has accumulated the proper actions and predisposition, so that when he receives initiation and the lama's identification of reality, he attains highest realization.
>
> The gradual mode, on the other hand, is not that of the sutra systems in which one achieves enlightenment only after countless aeons of practice, but that of someone on the mantra path who completes the auspicious qualities, finishing the grounds (bhumi) and paths (marga) gradually, even in one lifetime. However, when he identifies reality, he is unable to progress along these paths simultaneously but has to proceed in stages. Thus, even the gradual path is not necessarily long.

26. Although both Buddhists who have taken the lay precepts (*upasaka*) and monks are forbidden to drink, alcohol plays an important part in tantric rituals. It is said that one of the last obstacles to realization is the mind that holds to the dualistic concepts of purity and impurity. Consuming alcohol and meat during the tantric feast (ganachakra) with a non-dualistic view, is a way to break through this fixation.

However, it is also cautioned that one should drink no more than one skull-cup full of alcohol, and most lamas and monks will consume less than one drop of alcohol during ganachakras, as a token. Unless one possesses the capacity to truly transform alcohol as a tool, the would-be tantrika may wind up in the hell realms. See Tulku Thondup, *Enlightened Living*, pp. 132-138, for an excellent essay by Jigme Lingpa on this point. My own root guru,

Khenpo Karthar Rinpoche, commented, "When you can demonstrate magical siddhis like the three Khampas, then you can drink all you want! Until then, be careful!"

27. See note 25.

28. Milarepa demonstrated this siddhi to Rechungpa by climbing into a yak's horn to get out of the rain. The yak's horn grew no bigger, nor did Milarepa grow smaller. This served to curb Rechungpa's arrogance toward his teacher.

29. As I explained in my introduction to *Mahamudra: The Quintessence of Mind and Meditation*, by Takpo Tashi Namgyal, p. xxxvii:

> The history of mahamudra highlights the development of Tibetan Buddhism since its beginnings (Buddhism was introduced in Tibet during the seventh century C.E.). Tibetan Buddhism has synthesized many authentic Buddhist traditions while maintaining a dynamism and distinction all its own. Mahamudra—like the Nyingmapa's Mahasampanna [Dzogchen]—represents a special path that embodies a vision of the ultimate reality and an instantaneous self-realization process....The early Indian Buddhist teachers, starting from the second century C.E., preserved what was then designated as the "quintessence of reality." Gradually this was identified with the term "mahamudra." Among the enlightened teachers of the early period were Saraha, Nagarjuna, Savari, and Maitripa. Some great teachers of the later period included Tilopa and Naropa and their Tibetan disciples Marpa, Milarepa, and Gampopa. Their songs of enlightenment contain much of the mahamudra's wisdom. The doctrine on the quintessence of reality has remained a closely guarded secret....

During the eleventh and twelfth centuries the mahamudra doctrine attained a distinct position within the Kagyupa order in Tibet. According to the author of this treatise [Takpo Tashi Namgyal], it was the incomparable Gampopa who turned the mahamudra teaching into a special system of metaphysics and meditation, providing it with a strong foundation and institutional identity.

30. These include Karmapa's *Non-differentiation of Mind and Mental Energy (Lung Sem Yermay)*; Zhang's *Ultimate Path (Lamchok Tharthuk)*; Bahrampa's *The Hidden Path of Transmutation (Sepho Seblam)*; Phagdru's *The Secret Mantra (Sang Ngak)*; Taklungpa's *The Thirty-nine Principles of Liberation (Namthar Sogu)*; Drikungpa's *One Vital of The Three Vows (Domsum Naychik)*; Tsangpa Gyeray's *Interdependent Arising and Harmonization (Tendreldang Ronyom)*; and Logopa's *Revival and Renunciation (Mogudang Zhenlog)*.

31. It should be noted that Rinchen Zangpo (958-1055), the pre-eminent translator and leading figure in the Buddhist renaissance, reincarnated not long after his death, and his incarnation was the first to be recognized as such in Tibet. His nineteenth incarnation, Lochen Tulku, is alive today. Nonetheless, the first Karmapa was the first to establish the succession of leadership of an

order by reincarnation. Each successive Karmapa incarnation has been installed at Tsurphu Monastery as leader of the Karma Kagyu order.

32. The Third Jamgon Kongtrul passed away in 1992 in a tragic automobile accident in India.

33. The coming of Kyobpa Jigten Sumgon Ratnashri was prophesied by the Buddha in over twenty sutras and tantras. During his lifetime he gathered some 180,000 disciples around him, who later established 3,500 monasteries in India, China, and Tibet. In the nineteenth century, the renowned Rime master Jamgon Kongtrul said in his text, *The Treasury of Knowledge*, "The mountains are filled with Drikungpa practitioners, and all the plains are filled with Drikungpa patrons."

34. Of the *Gongchik*, the Drikung master, Khenpo Könchog Gyaltsen Rinpoche writes, "One of [Jigten Sumgon's] most famous works, the *Gong Chik*, contains all the essential aspects of Vinaya discipline, Bodhichitta, and tantra. This text has many commentaries, both detailed and concise, by such masters as Sherab Jungne, who was Lord Jigten Sumgon's own disciple, the Eighth Karmapa (Mikyo Dorje), the Fourth Shamarpa, and the Drikung Dharmakirti."

35. The name Taklung means "The Land of the Tiger."

36. The foremost teacher of the Shangpa Kagyu lineage in recent times was the great Kalu Rinpoche (1905-1989). Recognized as the activity incarnation of Jamgon Kongtrul Lodro Thaye, the great nineteenth century Rime teacher (see following footnote), Kalu Rinpoche became the senior meditation master of the Karma Kagyu, as well as being the main lineage holder of the Shangpa Kagyu. He first visited the West in 1972, and subsequently founded many meditation and retreat centers in Europe and North America, where his students completed the traditional three year retreat, training in both Shangpa and Karma Kagyu transmissions.

37. Throughout his life Kalu Rinpoche continued the work begun in his previous lifetime (as Jamgon Kongtrul Lodro Thaye), encouraging the non-sectarian spread of the practices and teachings of all lineages of Tibetan Buddhism.

38. Here, self-delusion refers to the deluded perception that there is a separate and inherently existing self. If there is a "self," there must logically be "other." Through our attempts to enhance and protect this false self, we commit all kinds of unwholesome acts with our body, speech, and mind. The negative karma thus produced binds us to the wheel of samsara, confused existence, and creates all the endless varieties of suffering. This self-delusion is the very foundation of dualistic thinking. The antidote is the cultivation of wisdom and compassion. Wisdom cures this delusion on the absolute level: by meditating on shunyata, or emptiness, we can gain a direct perception and experience of the emptiness of self (and other) that cuts through and liberates us from our entrenched habits of dualistic thinking. Thus we realize our inter-being with all life.

39. Past, present, and future.

40. Also known as the "twelve nidanas" and sometimes translated as the law of dependent origination. A fundamental doctrine of Buddhism, interdependent co-arising (pratitya-samutpada) describes all the various appearances in existence. Rather than seeing things as having unrelated, separate, independent, and inherent existence, all phenomena are seen as an interrelated network of phenomenal causes and results. See Glossary: *twelve links of interdependent origination*. For a detailed description and analysis of the twelve links of interdependent arising, see Gampopa's *Jewel Ornament of Liberation*, translated by H.V. Guenther, pp. 191-195; see also Kalu Rinpoche's *The Dharma*, pp. 15-23.

41. These terms are translated elsewhere in this book as the "generation stage" and the "completion stage." See the glossary for details.

42. On the Six Yogas of Naropa, see Garma C. C. Chang, *Teachings of Tibetan Yoga*, (now reprinted as *The Six Yogas of Naropa*, Snow Lion Publications). For the Six Yogas of Niguma, see the Second Dalai Lama and Glenn H. Mullin, *Selected Works of The Dalai Lama II: Tantric Yogas of Sister Niguma*.

43. See Milarepa's interaction with Geshe Tsakpuhwa, in Lobsang P. Lhalungpa, trans., *The Life of Milarepa*, chap. 9.

44. For a thorough explanation of the nine stages, see Lati Rinbochay et al., *Meditative States in Tibetan Buddhism*, pp. 52-91.

45. See Takpo Tashi Namgyal, *Mahamudra: The Quintessence of Mind and Meditation*, trans. Lobsang P. Lhalungpa, pp. 175-209.

46. There are various levels of understanding with regard to "emptiness" which have been elucidated within Buddhism. Rather than seeing these as conflicting, Tibetan Buddhist scholars and meditation masters present these as progressive levels of understanding, preparing one for the ultimate direct perception of emptiness, Buddhahood. For a complete explanation, see Khenpo Tsultrim Gyamtso Rimpoche, *Progressive Stages of Meditation on Emptiness*.

47. See Jeffrey Hopkins, *Compassion in Tibetan Buddhism*, p. 36.

48. See Takpo Tashi Namgyal, *Mahamudra: The Quintessence of Mind and Meditation*, p. 319.

49. In tantric practice, visualizing oneself as an enlightened deity or Buddha is essential. In quantum physics, modern psychology, as well as in shamanic practices around the world, it is recognized that intention shapes reality, and that, "As a person thinks, so they become." Tantra relies on this principle, and requires that one develop "vajra pride," indestructible confidence in ourselves as the deity during visualization. This is the key to awakening our Buddha potential, said to be latent within every sentient being in much the same way that an oak tree is latent within an acorn.

50. Higher levels of tantra emphasize the transformation of the passions into spiritual energy, the transformation of the duality of ordinary appearances into sacred form, and maintaining a non-dualistic view. With the emphasis very much on the absolute non-dualistic view of reality, it was common for less evolved tantrikas to scorn the moralistic Buddhist teachings of the relative level of teaching, and to flaunt their "transcendent perspective" by defying conventional morality. While there were a few "crazy mystics" who actually were able to transform the energies at this level and use unconventional behavior to benefit beings, more often than not it was just a rationalization for unevolved practitioners to indulge in libertinism. To minimize this kind of misunderstanding, tantra has traditionally been practiced in secret.

51. According to the Kagyupa Lama, Khenpo Könchog Gyaltsen Rinpoche (in a conversation with this author), Atisha did reveal the basic teachings of tantra to his disciples. However, in order to emphasize the Hinayana and Mahayana foundations of tantric practices, as well as to assure that those students progressing into higher tantra had the correct view and motivation, Atisha only revealed the rudiments of tantric practice, such as visualization of the deity and mantric repetition. He did not teach the "method path" of Highest Yoga Tantra, which emphasizes "tsa lung" or inner energy practices, such as the sexual yoga practices, the yoga of inner heat, and other practices of the Six Yogas of Naropa.

52. Keith Dowman, *Masters of Mahamudra*, pp. 5-6.

53. See Namgyal, *Mahamudra*, p. 271.

54. See Namgyal, *Mahamudra*, pp. 358-359.

54. Tantra requires that many strict vows or precept commitments (samaya) be strictly kept by the practitioner. Grave karmic consequences are said to occur to those who lack the will to maintain these vows. Therefore, many Buddhist practitioners were unwilling to seek initiation into tantra.

On Go Lotsawa's defense of Gampopa, see Jampa Thaye, *A Garland of Gold*, p. 18.

Glossary

Achala Miyowa in Tibetan, the remover of all obstacles, one of the enlightened deities.

acharya Master or teacher. Usually signifies accomplishment in both study and practice. See also *vajracharya*.

amrita Nectar, elixir of immortality. Blessed liquor used sacramentally during tantric ritual. Amrita symbolizes poison transformed into wisdom. It also helps to break through one's dualistic notions of pure and impure.

arhat One who has overcome the foe, foe destroyer. One who has overcome the obscurations of the four maras and has attained the final stage of the Hinayana path.

arura Arura is a name often used for the medicinal herb myrobalan, which is pictured in the right hand of the Medicine Buddha.

avadhuti The central energy channel of the illusory body or vajra body. The central channel begins at the tip of the penis in men and the tip of the clitoris in women. It ascends in a straight line to the crown of the head, and then arches forward and downward, ending at the mid-eyebrow point. It is blue in color and straight like an arrow. Inside it has an oily red color. It is clear and transparent, and is soft and flexible like a flower petal. It is the trunk of the energy body, and links the chakras together.

Avalokiteshvara The bodhisattva of compassion, Chenrezig in Tibetan. Avalokiteshvara is considered to be a historical person, one of Shakyamuni Buddha's main disciples. The Dalai Lamas of Tibet are considered to be nirmanakaya emanations of Avalokiteshvara, as are the Gyalwa Karmapas of the Karma Kagyu lineage.

bardo The intermediate state. Although bardo commonly refers to the state between death and rebirth, there are actually six bardos: (1) the bardo of dying; (2) the bardo of dharmata (the luminosity immediately following death);

(3) the bardo of becoming (where one is drawn toward rebirth); (4) the bardo of birth and death (life in one of the six realms); (5) the bardo of dreaming (the state between falling asleep and waking); (6) the bardo of meditation (samadhi).

Beghar A very powerful spirit who was subdued by Padmasambhava and made the guardian of Samye Monastery. Beghar is said to be the king of the spirit world. Some consider him an emanation of Amitabha. Beghar tests the resolve and purity of Dharma students. If the student is strongly established in his or her practice, Beghar can help them.

Bhagavan Blessed One. An epithet which usually refers to the Buddha. It is also used when referring to one's guru (who one sees as the Buddha), or when referring to a peaceful male yidam.

bhikshu A fully-ordained monk, one who has vowed to observe the 253 monastic precepts of the Vinaya. Today there is usually a waiting period between receiving novitiate ordination and full monastic ordination; but according to all the accounts, Gampopa received both novice and bhikshu ordination simultaneously.

bindu Drop, dot, semen, essence. The bindu or drops are about the size of sesame seeds, and are more substantive than prana. Although substantial, they are clear like a crystal or diamond, and magnificently bright. There are two basic types of drops: the white drops and the red drops. The white drops are the pure essence of the male seminal fluid (sperm). The red drops are related to the pure essence of the female menstrual blood (ovum). There are both gross and subtle aspects to the drops. The gross or substantive form of the red and white drops flow through the nadis or channels. The subtle drops exist within the center of the heart chakra which is penetrated by the central channel.

The seat of the white drop is in the crown chakra at the top of the head, and it is from here that the semen originates. The seat of the red drop is in the navel chakra, and it is from here that the blood originates. The red drop is also the source of bodily warmth, and is the foundation for developing the inner heat of tummo. The energy of the drops have both a temporary and an ultimate value. Their temporary value is to produce the state of great bliss for Highest Yoga Tantra practitioners. Within that experience of the blissful state, one uses the mind of great bliss to meditate on emptiness. This is the ultimate value, the realization of the yidam Chakrasamvara (or Hevajra, Kalachakra, Guhyasamaja), whose essential nature is skillful means inseparable from emptiness.

In some contexts, bindu refers specifically to the sexual essences, i.e. the semen and blood. Conservation of these substances is considered vital to Highest Yoga Tantra.

bodhichitta *Bodhi* means awakening, while *chitta* means mind. Thus bodhicitta means "the awakening mind." There are two types of bodhichitta, absolute or ultimate bodhichitta, and relative bodhichitta. According to

Gampopa, absolute bodhichitta is the non-dual realization of emptiness inseparable from compassion, which is radiant, unshakable and beyond concepts. Relative bodhichitta is the compassionate mind of the bodhisattva, which aspires and works to liberate all sentient beings from samsara through the practice of the six paramitas.

bodhisattva Awakening hero. One who is following the Mahayana path of the six paramitas and is cultivating bodhichitta, both relative and absolute. One formally takes the bodhisattva vow from one's spiritual master, and thereafter renews the vow daily with the aspiration to attain enlightenment not merely for oneself, but for the sake of all sentient beings, and to continue to be reborn within samsara until all beings have attained enlightenment.

bodhisattva path See bodhisattva stages.

bodhisattva posture The meditation position where the legs are loosely crossed, with the left leg drawn up close (symbolizing control of sexual energy), and the right leg slightly out in front (symbolizing the readiness to act for the benefit of sentient beings).

bodhisattva stages There are ten bodhisattva stages or bhumis: (1) The Joyous; (2) The Stainless; (3) The Radiant; (4) The Brilliant; (5) The Hard to Conquer; (6) The Realized; (7) The Reaching Far; (8) The Unshakable; (9) The Good Intelligence; (10) The Cloud of Dharma. At each stage, more defilements and obscurations are purified, and more enlightened qualities are manifested. The first six stages correspond to the realization of the six paramitas, and the last four to refinement of the perfection of wisdom (prajna paramita). The ten stages are progressive, but do not always occur in a linear fashion. Beyond the tenth stage is complete awakening, buddhahood.

buddha field The realm or abode of a Buddha.

buddha nature The potential for enlightenment that is inherent in all sentient beings; the true nature of mind.

buddhahood Complete and perfect enlightenment.

bhumi Ground, stage, level. The levels or stages of realization on the bodhisattva path. See *bodhisattva stages*.

Catuhpitha Four seats. A mother tantra of the Highest Yoga Tantra class, associated with the vajra family.

central channel See *avadhuti*.

chakra Circle, wheel. The energetic centers in the core of the body linked together by the central channel. The seven chakras are: (1) base chakra; (2) navel chakra; (3) solar plexus chakra; (4) heart chakra; (5) throat chakra; (6) third eye chakra; and (7) crown chakra.

Chakrasamvara A semi-wrathful (blissful) Heruka of the padma or lotus family, belonging to the class of mother tantras. Blue in color, he is usually depicted in union with his female consort, Vajrayogini, who is red. He is the principal deity of the Kagyu lineage, and is also very important to the Gelugpas.

chang Tibetan barley beer.

Chod Literally, to cut. In the yogic context, it means to cut the basis of attachment to the illusion of a separate and inherently existing self through the ritual offering of one's body to all beings; and to cut the four maras in particular.

The Chod practice is based upon the revelations of the *Prajnaparamita Sutras*. It was introduced into Tibet by the Indian guru Phadampa Sangye, and was developed by his chief Tibetan disciple, the great Tibetan yogini Machig Labdron. Machig Labdron became so renowned that students and teachers travelled from India to Tibet to receive her Chod teachings.

Because of the shamanistic character of the Chod practice, some have speculated that it was adopted from Bon, the pre-Buddhist religion of Tibet. However, according to Lopon Tenzin Namdak, the current head of the Bonpo tradition, they also learned Chod from Phadampa Sangye, and made it a part of their tradition at the same time as the Buddhists.

clear light The experience of the true, unfabricated, and uncontrived nature of mind, present throughout all of samsara and nirvana. There are two aspects to clear light: empty clear light, which is like a clear open sky; and manifest clear light, which appears as the five lights, images, and the like.

completion stage One of the two main stages of tantric practice. In the completion stage of Mahamudra, one dissolves the visualization of the deity and mandala established in the generation stage, and does formless meditation on the non-dual nature of mind.

"Completion stage with signs" refers to the highest levels of tantric practice, where the emphasis is on working with the prana, nadis, and bindu. The goal is to change ones karmapranas into jnanapranas, transforming one's ordinary body, speech, and mind into the body, speech, and mind of a Buddha. This phase of practice is also called tsa-lung, meaning nadi-prana or channel-wind practice; it is the central focus of all Six Yogas of Naropa. Tsa-lung practice requires prior mastery of the generation stage to achieve success.

"Completion stage without signs" refers to the practice of Essence Mahamudra, which is the essential view of Mahamudra, introduced directly to the student without dependence on intellectual or philosophical reasoning.

co-emergence, co-emergent wisdom See *sahaja*.

daka Sky-goer, hero, warrior. A male semi-wrathful yidam. One of the three roots of tantric refuge, dakas are beings who are related to enlightened activity and skillful means. They may also be messengers or protectors, depending on the context. There are both worldly and enlightened dakas.

dakini Sky-goer. A female yidam. Although they are usually depicted as wrathful or semi-wrathful, they can also be peaceful, as in the case of Yeshe Tsogyal, Padmasambhava's consort. They symbolize wisdom and emptiness, the basic, fertile space of wisdom out of which both samsara and nirvana arise. They can be playful and tricky, even dangerous, yet their essence is compassionate. There are both worldly and enlightened dakinis.

Dakpo Lhaje The Physician from Dakpo. Dakpo refers to the region where Gampopa set up his monastery, at Mount Gampo Dar, in the latter part of his life (hence the name Gampopa, the man from Gampo.) Gampopa is often referred to as Dakpo Lhaje, Dakpopa, or Dakpo Rinpoche. His lineage is also known as the Dakpo Kagyu.

damaru A two-headed hand-held drum used in Vajrayana ritual.

Desire Realm One of three realms of existence within samsara, comprised of the gods, demi-gods, humans, animals, hungry ghosts, and hell beings. It is called the Desire Realm because beings are reborn and experience suffering within this realm due to gross attachment and desire. See also *Form Realm* and *Formless Realm*.

Dharma Truth, law, way, path. The teachings of the Buddhas. In other contexts "dharma" refers to phenomena or mental and physical objects.

dharmadhatu The unborn realm of all-encompassing space in which all things arise, exist, and cease.

dharmakaya See *four bodies of a buddha*.

dharmata Suchness. The pure nature of reality, phenomena, and mind as they are, without elaboration.

doha Spontaneous verse sung by Vajrayana practitioners as an expression of their realization and instruction. Milarepa is famous for his doha compositions, yet many other Indian and Tibetan masters have also composed brilliant and inspiring dohas.

eight worldly dharmas The eight worldly dharmas are: gain and loss, pleasure and pain, fame and infamy, praise and scorn.

Dombhi Dombhi was one of the eighty-four mahasiddhas of the Indian Mahamudra lineage. A king of Magadha, Dombhi was initiated into the mandala of Hevajra by the mahasiddha Virupa. Although he was an enlightened ruler who brought peace to his nation, Dombhi was forced to abdicate for choosing a lower caste woman as his tantric consort. After his departure the country fell into misgovernment and longed for their old ruler back. Summoned to return from his jungle retreat, Dombhi emerged from the jungle astride a pregnant tigress, waving a poisonous snake as a whip, to demonstrate his attainments.

empowerment The three prerequisites for tantric practice are: empowerment or initiation into the particular tantra; the oral transmission blessing, in the form of a ritual reading of the tantric sadhana to be practiced; and the oral pith-instructions on how to correctly perform the practice.

During an empowerment, the Vajra master goes into the various samadhis required in the practice, wherein he energetically and symbolically transmits the experience—the fruit of the practice—to the initiate. The initiate is usually unable to sustain the peak of this experience, but this transmission blessing plants a seed, or experiential frame of reference, to be deepened through continued practice, until the experience is finally stabilized and ripens into full perfect realization.

emptiness The teaching that self and all phenomena are empty of, or lack, inherent and independent existence.

five elements Fire, earth, air, water, and space.

five lay precepts Vows, taken by lay-people, to refrain from: (1) killing, (2) stealing, (3) lying, (4) sexual misconduct, and (5) alcohol and intoxicating drugs.

food of samadhi A level of meditation where one is so absorbed in meditative concentration that one needs no food.

Form Realm A god realm where the beings are free from the desires of the Desire Realm, but still have attachment to subtler forms and sensations. There is neither taste nor smell in the Form Realm. The beings reborn here have cultivated various meditative absorptions; they are huge and live extremely long lives.

Formless Realm The highest god realms, where beings have cut off attachment to both the Desire and Form Realm objects, but are still fixated on the bliss of meditation. They have no bodies, since they have transcended form.

four bodies of a Buddha The four bodies or four kayas of the Buddha are: (1) the dharmakaya or ultimate truth body, corresponding to the mind aspect of the Buddha; (2) the sambhogakaya or complete enjoyment body, corresponding to the speech and prana aspect of the Buddha; (3) the nirmanakaya, the emanation body, corresponding to the physical human body of the Buddha; and, (4) the svabhavikakaya, the essential or nature body, representing the inseparability of the first three Bodies.

Sometimes only two kayas are mentioned: the dharmakaya, and the rupakaya or form body. In this instance, the rupakaya encompasses both the sambhogakaya and the nirmanakaya. These are sometimes spoken of in the context of the "two benefits": one realizes the ultimate non-dual truth body of dharmakaya for one's own benefit; and one realizes the relative manifestations of the rupakaya in order to benefit all sentient beings.

four generosities The four generosities are: Giving material goods such as food and alms, giving loving-kindness, giving refuge from fear, and sharing the Dharma teachings.

four immeasurables The four immeasurables are: Loving kindness, the desire to see all beings happy; compassion, the desire to see all beings free from suffering; joy in the joy of others; equanimity, caring equally for all beings without partiality.

four initiations The four initiations are the four major empowerments given within a tantric initiation: (1) the vase empowerment, blessing one's body to become Buddha's body, and planting the seed to realize the nirmanakaya; (2) the secret empowerment, blessing one's speech to become Buddha's speech, and planting the seed to attain the sambhogakaya; (3) the wisdom empowerment, blessing one's mind to become Buddha's mind, and planting the seed to realize the dharmakaya; (4) the precious word empowerment, blessing one's body, speech, and mind to become inseparable from the state of Vajradhara, and planting the seed to realize the svabhavikakaya, the ultimate realization of suchness.

four maras Four of the major obstacles to spiritual practice and enlightenment. These are: (1) skandha-mara, falsely perceiving the five skandhas as an inherently existing self; (2) klesha-mara, being overcome by the mental confusion of conflicting emotions; (3) mrtyu-mara, death, which causes a break in spiritual practice unless the practitioner is able to use the experience of dying to achieve enlightenment; (4) devaputra-mara, the "mara of the gods' son," where life becomes so pleasurable that one is distracted from spiritual practice.

four powers The four steps used to purify and eliminate negative karma: (1) the power of confession, where one admits negative actions of body, speech, and mind committed in this life and in all prior lives; (2) the power of regret, where one understands the suffering and negative karma one has created, and sincerely regrets having committed the action; (3) the power of resolution, firmly resolving never to repeat the action again, even at the cost of one's life; (4) the power of reliance, praying to the buddhas and bodhisattvas for help and support in one's effort to abandon all negative karma.

four transmissions Tilopa, the father of the Kagyu lineage, received four sets of yogic practice from several gurus, which he in turn transmitted to his disciple, Naropa. These four transmissions are often said to be: the illusory body yoga, dream yoga, clear light or luminosity yoga, and tummo or candali yoga. These became the main source of the Six Yogas of Naropa. For a different account of the four transmissions, see Nalanda and Chogyam Trungpa, *The Life of Marpa the Translator*, pp. xxxii-xxxiii.

Gampo Dar Mount Gampo Dar is the location where Gampopa established his monastery, and it is the source of his name, Gampopa, "the man from Gampo." Gampo means calm, sober, deep. Khenpo Karthar Rinpoche says, "Of all the places in Tibet, Gampo Dar has the most breathtaking scenery."

ganachakra A gathering of tantric practitioners for a sacred ritual feast, called "tsog kyi khor lo" or "tsog" in Tibetan.

Ge Lugha A historical giant and Herculean warrior.

generation stage The first of the two main stages of tantric practice, wherein one's relative perceptions of reality are purified through mudra, mantra, and visualization of the deity. This serves to eliminate one's negative habitual tendencies of mind, and prepares one for the completion stage. See also *completion stage*.

Guhyasamaja The most important father tantra of Highest Yoga Tantra. Guhyasamaja belongs to the vajra family of the five buddha families, and represents the power of anger transformed into mirror-like wisdom. Blue in color, he is usually depicted with six arms and four faces. Guhyasamaja was one of Marpa's special practices.

guru See *lama*.

guru yoga The most important daily tantric practice, wherein one visualizes one's spiritual teacher in the center of the mandala, supplicates him, receives empowerments, blessings, and siddhis from him, and ultimately merges one's own mind inseparably with his. One must see the guru as none other than a fully realized Buddha to experience the full power and blessings of guru yoga.

The different lineages have different visualizations of the guru. In the Kagyu lineage, one visualizes the guru either in the form of Vajradhara or in the form of the founders of the particular branch of the Kagyu lineage. In the Karma Kagyu, the guru is usually visualized in the form of the Karmapa. There are also special guru yogas of the founding Kagyu fathers: Marpa, Milarepa, and Gampopa. In the Nyingma lineages, generally one visualizes one's guru in the form of Padmasambhava.

heart energy-wind One of the five main energy-winds or pranas. Also called the "life supporting wind," it is seated in the heart and spine, and is the mother of all the other winds in the body.

Heruka A wrathful male yidam, symbolizing the masculine principles of skillful means and energy. The Tibetan name, "trag thung," signifies one who drinks the blood of clinging to self. Chakrasamvara, Hevajra, and Hayagriva are some examples of Herukas. Heruka also refers to the wrathful and semi-wrathful deities who appear in the bardo of dharmata after death.

Hevajra A semi-wrathful (ecstatic or blissful) male Heruka. One of the major yidams of both the Kagyupa and Sakyapa lineages. Hevajra was the main yidam of Marpa the Translator. Hevajra is blue in color, and appears in four, six, and twelve armed forms, in blissful union with his female consort, Nairatmya. The Hevajra Tantra is one of the main cycles of Buddhist tantra.

Highest Yoga Tantra The highest of the four classes of tantra, according to the New Translation schools.

Hinayana The Hinayana teachings are the sutras taught by Siddhartha Gautama, the historical Buddha, to the monks and lay people who followed him. One collection of these scriptures was later recorded in writing as the Pali Canon. The Hinayana tradition includes many of the Buddha's basic teachings, such as the Vinaya or rules of moral discipline for monks and lay people, the Four Noble Truths on the origin and cessation of suffering, the Noble Eightfold Path on the right way of life, and the *Dhammapada*.

Although the virtues of loving-kindness and compassion are taught within the Hinayana, meditation, mindfulness, non-attachment, and strict moral discipline are emphasized as the keys to developing penetrating wisdom, which would lead one to nirvana or liberation from suffering. The Hinayana is often referred to as "the path of renunciation," and those who accomplish this path attain to the level of Arhatship by means of the path of the Hearer (Shravaka) or that of a Solitary Realizer (Pratyekabuddha).

illusory body In an ordinary being it refers to the subtle body composed of nadis, prana, and bindu. In an accomplished yogi who has refined the nadis, prana, and bindu, the illusory body becomes the basis for the rupakaya. It is also called the rainbow body or vajra body. See also *four bodies of a Buddha* and *vajra body.*

initiation See *empowerment* and *four initiations.*

innate co-emergent awareness See *sahaja.*

Jetsun Venerable, reverend. A Tibetan honorific term used in addressing highly respected masters.

jnanaprana Wisdom energy, wisdom wind. Prana is the source of all movement, including the movement of mind. The quality of one's mind depends upon the prana or wind on which it is mounted. If the prana is impure, the mind riding it will necessarily be impure as well. If the prana is a wisdom wind, the mind riding that prana will be a wisdom mind. The pranas moving within the central channel are wisdom winds. Since the realization of wisdom depends upon wisdom winds, yogis produce wisdom consciousness by moving all their winds into the central channel.

Kadampa is the name given to the lineage established by Atisha in Tibet. It was later integrated into the Kagyupa school by Gampopa, and was the foundation of the Gelugpa lineage of the Dalai Lamas.

kapala A cup or bowl made of a human skull. Used in Vajrayana ritual, the kapala has numerous levels of symbolism. On one level it is a reminder of inevitable death, and goads one to use one's time to practice the Dharma fervently. On a higher level it leads one to transcend one's dualistic concepts of pure or impure, clean or unclean, good and evil.

karma Action. The universal law that what we experience now is a result of our previous actions of body, speech, and mind; and what we experience in the future will be determined by our current actions. Karma is subdivided into positive, negative and neutral, stemming from wholesome, unwholesome, and neutral acts.

One seeks to cultivate positive karma in order to provide beneficial circumstances for the practice of Dharma, and to purify negative karma in order to eliminate obstacles to practice. However, ultimate liberation from samsara is the result of insight and discipline, and can not be gained merely by positive karma; positive karma simply serves to create a fertile field wherein one is more likely to encounter Dharma and to have the predilection and propensity to practice.

karmamudra Action seal. A yogic consort or tantric sexual partner.

karmaprana Impure winds. The pranas moving in the left and right channels, as well as in the rest of the 72,000 channels, are impure karmapranas, or winds giving birth to dualistic concepts. They perpetuate the concept of a separate, inherently existing self. From this fundamental fixation on self we create the idea of others; we divide others into friends, enemies, and those to whom we are indifferent; from this we develop the three poisons of attachment, aggression, and ignorance. Thus we develop and perpetuate our existence in samsara. See also *jnanaprana*.

kayas See *four bodies of a Buddha*.

khatvanga The khatvanga staff is an ornament of many tantric deities. It is usually held in the crook of the left elbow. It represents the sacred consort, and the inseparability of wisdom and skillful means. The khatvanga is adorned with a five-pointed vajra and three severed heads: a freshly severed head, a dried head, and a skull. The five-pointed vajra symbolizes vanquishing the five poisons of pride, jealousy, greed, hatred, and ignorance, and the attainment of the five transcendent wisdoms. The three human heads represent attainment of the three kayas.

khenpo means abbot or preceptor.

lalana Moon channel, lunar channel, object channel. This is the main left channel, white in color. It intersects the central channel at the tip of the sex organ. As it ascends, it separates slightly to the left of the central channel and rejoins it at the navel. From the navel to the crown it runs parallel and adjacent to the central channel. At the crown of the head it separates again to the left and terminates at the left nostril.

The left channel is related to the nirmanakaya in its pure state, and to the conflicting emotion of desire in its afflicted state. In some tantras, the qualities and colors of the left and right channels are reversed for women, as men and women are considered to have opposite internal energy structures.

Lam Rim or Gradual Stages of the Path to Enlightenment is a system of teaching and meditation initially introduced into Tibetan Buddhism by Atisha. This approach integrates all the teachings of the three yanas (Hinayana, Mahayana, and Vajrayana) into one progressive system of training and realization on the path to Buddhahood.

lama The term "lama" can apply to both monastic and lay teachers. It has the meaning of "teacher-mother," implying that the teacher who gives spiritual teachings that can guide one to Buddhahood is showing kindness as great as one's mother. In the Kagyu tradition it is a title usually reserved for those who have completed the traditional three-year, three-month, and three-day retreat.

left channel See *lalana.*

Luipa One of the eighty-four Indian mahasiddhas. His teachings were passed down through Tilopa and Naropa, and brought to Tibet by Marpa, who passed them on to Milarepa.

luminosity See *clear light.*

Mahamudra A term virtually synonymous with Buddhahood. It means the "Great Seal" or "Sublime Stance," the spontaneous embodiment of the all-knowing wisdom and limitless compassion of a Buddha. Mahamudra is also the name of the specific systems of spiritual practice inherited by the Tibetans from the Indian mahasiddhas.

Mahayana Great Vehicle. The Mahayana teachings were first revealed by Arya Nagarjuna between the first and second century C.E., in south India. The legends say that Nagarjuna, who is sometimes called the "second Buddha," traveled to the realm of the nagas or water serpents, and there retrieved the Mahayana teachings of Buddha, which had been entrusted to the nagas' safekeeping until the world was ready to receive them.

These teachings were named the Great Vehicle (to enlightenment) because of the greatness of the aspirations of its followers, in contrast to that of the Hinayana or "Lesser Vehicle."

This great aspiration is characterized by the path of the bodhisattva, which has been described by E. A. Burtt, "...the bodhisattva has transcended the state in which he is concerned for his own salvation; he is committed to the eternal weal of all living beings, and will not rest until he has led them all to the goal. On attaining enlightenment he does not leave the world behind and enter nirvana by himself; he remains in the world, appearing like an ordinary person, but devoting his compassionate skill to the aid of others. He shares and bears the burden of their sufferings, in loving union with them, instead of merely giving others an example of a person who has overcome the causes of suffering for himself." (*The Teachings of the Compassionate Buddha*, p. 130).

For this reason the Mahayana is often called "the path of compassion." By following the path of the bodhisattva the goal of Buddhahood or full and total spiritual awakening, equal to that of the historical Buddha, can be attained.

mala A rosary, usually with 108 beads, used to count mantra recitations. One round of the mala is counted as an even one hundred recitations, under the assumption that one's mind may have been distracted at some point during the round, so one adds an extra eight for good measure.

mandala The deity and his or her surrounding environment, often visualized or depicted in thangkas and sand paintings. It is usually constructed with a center and four gates, representing the four cardinal directions. One may also present a mandala representing the entire universe, with Mount Meru in the center, as an offering to the Three Jewels, in order to accumulate merit; this type of mandala is visualized, and can also be represented through mudra or through heaps of rice on a plate.

mantra Mantras are Sanskrit syllables or words that are used to invoke the speech or energy qualities of a particular deity. It is unnecessary for the practitioner to know the meaning of the words, because the sound of the mantra itself helps to transform one's energy and thus one's awareness. Because of its relationship to breath, speech, and prana, mantra recitation can activate the jnanapranas and help to suspend the activities of the karmapranas. Mantra is always conjoined with visualization and mudra within a tantric sadhana. The vehicle of the Tantrayana is also referred to as the Mantrayana.

mara See *four maras.*

Medicine Buddha The buddha associated with healing, on both the spiritual and physical levels. He is blue in color, and holds a begging bowl full of medicine in his left hand, and a myrobalan (arura) flower in his right hand.

method path This refers to the Six Yogas of Naropa, wherein, through meditation on the channels, winds, and drops, one transforms ordinary body, speech, and mind into the three vajras: vajra body, vajra speech, and vajra mind. It also refers to the generation and completion stage "with signs" (see *completion stage*).

Another meaning of "method" is great bliss. In contrast to other paths, which may emphasize the direct experience of wisdom through a penetrating realization of emptiness, the method path of Vajrayana emphasizes the union of wisdom and method, that is, the union of wisdom simultaneous with great bliss.

Mon is a place at the border of Tibet and Bhutan.

mother and son luminosities Mother luminosity refers to the primordially self-existing luminosity. The son luminosity refers to the yogi's various experiences of luminosity along the stages of the path. When they are united, this refers to the meditator's ultimate realization of luminosity.

mudra Gesture, seal, sign, symbol. Mudra generally refers to the hand gestures during Vajrayana practices that symbolize the qualities, moods, and actions related to a specific yidam. Vajrayana practice incorporates one's body, speech, and mind into the practice. Mudra corresponds to the body, drawing it into sacred activity. Mudra thus supports mantra and samadhi in the process of invoking the yidam.

See *karmamudra* and *Mahamudra* for other uses of the term.

nadi These are the pathways of the illusory body through which the prana and bindu flow. The three most important nadis in Highest Yoga Tantra are the avadhuti (central channel), the lalana (left channel), and the rasana (right channel). These channels subdivide and eventually form a network of 72,000 channels pervading the entire body. See also *prana* and *bindu.*

nectar See *amrita.*

New Moonlight Healer The name of Gampopa in a previous life, when he was a bodhisattva at the time of Buddha Shakyamuni: Tsoje Dawo Shunu in Tibetan, Chandraprabhava-kumara in Sanskrit. The full moon symbolizes complete enlightenment or Buddhahood. The light of the new or waxing moon symbolizes the realization of a bodhisattva, one who is partially illuminated and is on the path to complete spiritual realization.

Nirmanakaya See *four bodies of a Buddha.*

one taste Realization of the non-dual nature of mind and phenomenon. One of the four yogas of Mahamudra.

paramita See *six paramitas.*

pith-instructions The personal communication of the essence of a meditation practice from guru to student. Through this direct communication both the literal meaning and the intuitive sense are transmitted to a receptive disciple, since merely being in the field of a guru who has personally realized the practice conveys a powerful and subtle non-verbal message. The guru also adapts his presentation to the capacity, individual needs, and ripeness of the student in the moment. Meditations learned from books are considered useless without receiving the oral instructions from a guru. Because of its firm emphasis on the orally transmitted pith-instructions being passed from teacher to student, the Kagyu lineage is also known as the "hearing lineage."

prajna Wisdom.

prana Wind, vital airs, energy. Prana is the life-force energy that flows through the channels (nadis) of the illusory body. Prana is the foundation of all movement and thus of all vital bodily functions. Prana is the bridge between the body and the mind. It is likened to a horse, with the mind as the rider and the nadis as the road. It corresponds to speech, breath, mantra, and to realization of the sambhogakaya. There are both pure and impure pranas (see *karmaprana* and *jnanaprana*). See also *nadi* and *bindu*.

pranayama Yogic breathing exercises designed to direct body, prana, and mind.

Pure Land It often refers to the buddha field of Buddha Amitabha, known as the Pure Land of Great Bliss, Dewachen. But it can also refer to other buddha fields, or pure places where Buddhas abide.

puja Offering ritual or ceremony of worship.

Rahu Hindu mythology speaks of nine planets. Rahu is depicted as a demon whose head was severed from his body by Vishnu. These two parts of his body became the eighth and ninth planets, Rahu and Ketu. Rahu is the celestial body said to be responsible for eclipses by swallowing the sun and the moon.

refuge One formally becomes a Buddhist when one takes refuge in the Three Jewels: the Buddha as the teacher or guide, the Dharma as the teaching or path, and the Sangha or excellent community as one's companions on the journey. In tantra, one adds taking refuge in the Three Roots: the guru as the root of all blessings, the yidam or meditational deity as the root of all attainment, and the dharmapalas or protector deities as the root of all enlightened activity.

rasana This is the main right energy channel, blue in color. It intersects with the central channel at the tip of the sex organ. As it ascends, it separates slightly to the right of the central channel and rejoins it at the navel. From the navel to the crown it runs parallel and adjacent to the central channel. At the crown it separates again to the right and terminates at the right nostril.

The right channel is related to the sambhogakaya in its pure state, and to the conflicting emotion of anger or aversion in its afflicted state. See also *lalana*.

repa Tibetan for "cotton-clad ones." It refers to followers of the tantric yogi path who practice the inner heat or tummo yoga. To demonstrate their mastery of the inner heat, their only garment is a lightweight cotton robe, even in the midst of the fierce Tibetan winter.

right channel See *rasana*.

Rime (pronounced Ree-may) was a movement for intersectarian harmony and cooperation, rekindled and revitalized in the nineteenth century by several of Tibet's greatest masters. Led by Jamgon Kongtrul Lodro Thaye, the greatest scholar and eclectic master of the time, he and others collected and compiled the complete teachings, transmissions, empowerments, and meditation practices from all the various orders of Tibetan Buddhism. This collection was called The Five Great Treasures. Their goal was to eliminate the sectarian divisions and often bitter rivalry among the various schools, and to revivify the emphasis on the actual practice of the teachings.

Rinpoche Precious One. An honorific term reserved for tulkus or lamas of high rank or great meditative accomplishment.

sacred outlook The essential view of Vajrayana practice. The tantric practitioner seeks to maintain the pure perceptions of an enlightened being, wherein one's environment is viewed as a Buddha field; all beings appear in the form of one's yidam or as Buddhas, bodhisattvas, dakas and dakinis; all sound is perceived as mantra; and all that arises in the mind is perceived as inseparable from emptiness.

In the Vajrayana view, maintaining sacred outlook is considered to be seeing into the true nature of reality and not merely idealistic projection. It helps us to cut through our ordinary distorted fixations on the nature of reality and to see things as they truly are.

Sadaprarudita The story of Sadaprarudita searching for his guru is related in the last chapters of the *Prajnaparamita Sutras*.

sadhana This term refers both to tantric ritual texts and to the practices presented in those texts.

sahaja Produced together, co-emergent wisdom. As Keith Dowman explains this term, "From the beginning the ultimate and relative, the male and female principles, form and emptiness, have arisen simultaneously; the inborn absolute [i.e. sahaja] is inherent in every instant of sensory experience, and it remains for the sadhaka to recognize it. However, this is not so easy as the degenerate, latter-day Bengali sahaja-yogi school with its concepts of 'natural enlightenment' and 'no practice' would believe; such notions make mockery of the siddha's sadhanas." (*Masters of Mahamudra*, pp. 421-422)

Saltong Shogum One of Gampopa's foremost disciples, from Kham. Sal means "clear" and Tong is short for Tong Pa Nyid, meaning "emptiness," indicating that he was born with the realization of emptiness and clear luminosity. Shogum means "harelip," because he was born with a cleft palate. Saltong Shogum became the guru who founded the Traleg Kyabgon line of tulkus, the supreme abbots of Thrangu Monastery in Kham.

samadhi Meditative concentration or absorption, when the meditation and the mind of the meditator become inseparable.

samaya Sacred vow or commitment. At each level of entry into the Buddhist path there are specific commitments which one vows to uphold. There is refuge ordination, the five lay precepts, the bodhisattva vow, monastic ordination, and tantra, and each stage has specific samayas. Also, when one receives tantric initiation from a vajra master into the mandala of a particular deity, one often receives a specific samaya associated with that practice. In general, the samaya of the Hinayana is to cause no harm to any sentient being; for the Mahayana the samaya is to help all sentient beings; for the Vajrayana the samaya is to retain sacred outlook. The most important samaya in tantra is to retain a pure relationship with one's guru.

sambhogakaya See *four bodies of a Buddha*.

samsara Cyclic existence, wheel of life and death. The state of ordinary beings experiencing suffering in the six realms of transmigratory existence due to primordial ignorance.

sangha Sangha means the "excellent community." In the early days of Buddhism, the term was only applied to the ordained community of monks and nuns. It was later expanded to include lay disciples who had taken refuge in the Three Jewels: the Buddha, the Dharma, and the Sangha. In the Mahayana teachings, it can also be applied to include the mahasangha or "great community" of all sentient beings, in much the same sense that Native Americans refer to the myriad forms of creation as "all my relations."

Seven Branch Prayer Used in all lineages of Tibetan Buddhism to develop bodhichitta, the mind of enlightenment, and to accumulate merit. The seven parts of the prayer are: (1) to prostrate and pay homage, either physically or mentally, to all Buddhas and bodhisattvas in the universe; (2) to make actual and visualized offerings to the Buddhas and bodhisattvas; (3) to confess all one's wrongdoings and one's violations of vows and precepts; (4) to rejoice in the virtuous conduct of all beings; (5) to pray that the Dharma continues to be present and taught to all beings in accordance with their capacity to understand; (6) to beseech the Buddhas not to pass into nirvana yet, but to remain in samsara and teach until all beings are enlightened; (7) to dedicate the merit of one's practice toward one's own enlightenment in order to be able to guide all sentient beings to a similar level of attainment. The Seven Branch Prayer can be practiced on its own or in short form as a preliminary prayer for other practices.

seven aryan riches Arya means "superior being," one who has had a direct experience of ultimate truth. The seven riches of a bodhisattva, one on the path to ultimate awakening, are: faith, discipline, generosity, learning, moral behavior, modesty, and knowledge.

shamatha Calm abiding. The meditation practice of calming the mind so that it can focus unwaveringly on the object of meditation. There are nine levels of shamatha, which prepare one for the practice of vipashyana or insight meditation.

Shi Tro The tantras of the peaceful and wrathful deities, a special Nyingmapa cycle of teachings composed by Guru Rinpoche (Padmasambhava) and written down by his consort, Yeshe Tsogyal. The text (containing, among many other books, *The Tibetan Book of the Dead*) was buried in the earth to be found at a later time. It is one of the many terma or "treasures" that Guru Rinpoche hid throughout Tibet. It was discovered by Karma Lingpa, who was the incarnation of Guru Rinpoche's close disciple, Lotsawa Lui Gyaltsen.

Short Ah Tummo Yoga This short AH is visualized in the navel area for the purpose of igniting the inner fire or tummo. This is one of the completion stage yogas of Highest Yoga Tantra. For further reading see Geshe Kelsang Gyatso, *Clear Light of Bliss*, pp. 33-66. For a concise description of the practice see Kathleen MacDonald, *How To Meditate*, pp. 134-138.

shravaka Hearer. A practitioner of the Hinayana path, noted for living in communities with other Hinayana followers.

siddhi Psychic powers. There are two levels of powers or siddhis that come from doing intensive meditation: ordinary siddhis, which refer to miraculous powers such as levitation, flight, invisibility, the ability to create multiple images of oneself or to change form; and extraordinary siddhis, which mean full enlightenment, the perfection of wisdom and compassion. See also *six psychic powers*.

sindura mandala A mandala drawn on a mirror or polished silver surface covered with sindura, a powder made of red lead, vermillion or cinnabar. In some traditions the red powder would be made of dried menstrual blood.

Six Dharmas of Mahamudra See *Six Yogas of Naropa*.

six paramitas Also known as the Six Perfections or Six Transcendent Virtues. Cultivation of the six paramitas is the basis of the Mahayana, the path of the bodhisattva. The six paramitas are: generosity, patience, ethics or moral discipline, joyous effort or diligence, meditative concentration, and wisdom.

six psychic powers The six psychic powers or siddhis are: (1) thought reading; (2) memory of past lives; (3) clairaudience, by which all languages including those of birds and animals can be understood, from both near and far; (4) clairvoyance, particularly the intuition of the suffering and needs of others; (5) the ability to perform miracles, such as manipulating the elements, flight, walking on water, and so forth; (6) the ability to stop the five passions.

six realms The six dimensions of samsaric existence within the Desire Realm: (1) the god (deva) realm, brought about by pride; (2) the fighting or jealous god (asura) realm, brought about by jealousy or envy; (3) the human realm, brought about by desire; (4) the animal realm, brought about by ignorance and stupidity; (5) the hungry ghost (preta) realm, brought about by greed; (6) the hell realm, brought about by hatred and aggression. The first three worlds are known as the upper realms of samsara, and the last three are known as the lower realms.

The Six Treatises of the Kadampas are: The *Buddhajataka* or the *Jataka Tales*, the collection of stories of the Buddha's former lifetimes; one excellent English version is *The Hungry Tigress: Buddhist Legends and Jataka Tales* as told by Rafe Martin, Berkeley: Parallax Press, 1990. The *Dharmapada* (Pali: *Dhammapada*); numerous fine translations are available in English. The *Bodhisattvacharyavatara*, by Shantideva; several translations exist in English, including, *A Guide to the Bodhisattva's Way of Life*, translated by Stephen Batchelor. The *Shikshasamuchaya*; the *Bodhisattvabhumi*; and the *Shravakabhumi*.

Six Yogas of Naropa Also called the Six Dharmas of Naropa, they are completion stage yogas of Highest Yoga Tantra: the yoga of inner heat; the yoga of the illusory body; the yoga of the dream state; the yoga of the bardo; the yoga of the clear light; and the yoga of the transference of consciousness at death.

skandha Aggregate, heap. The five skandhas are form, sensation, conception, mental formation, and, consciousness. The five aggregates are the physical and mental components of a human being. Due to ignorance we mistakenly assume that the skandhas, singly or collectively, have inherent concrete self-existence. When we actually examine them we find no inherently existing self. Yet there is no self apart from the five skandhas. In the *Heart Sutra*, the bodhisattva Avalokiteshvara expressed his realization of this paradox by proclaiming, "Form is no other than emptiness, emptiness is no other than form."

stupa Originally a reliquary containing the relics of the Buddha, later stupas were built to hold relics of other enlightened beings, scriptures, and statues as well. Stupas symbolize the dharmakaya, and range in size from small altar pieces to large monuments the size of buildings.

shunyata See *emptiness.*

sutra The recorded discourses attributed to Shakyamuni Buddha. In Tibet these works comprised the Kangyur texts. Sutra can also refer to the "causal path," as compared to tantra, the "path of results."

tantra Tantra generally refers to the fundamental texts of the Vajrayana, and to the systems of meditation described therein. Vajrayana is divided into four levels of tantra: Action (Kriya Tantra); Performance (Charya Tantra); Union (Yoga Tantra); and Highest Union or Highest Yoga Tantra (Anuttara-yoga Tantra). Tantra works on simultaneously transforming the three aspects of one's ordinary body, speech, and mind into the transcendent body, speech, and mind of a Buddha, through mudra, mantra, and visualization.

Because of its many skillful methods of practice, tantric Buddhism is often called "the short path" to enlightenment. It is possible to attain complete Buddhahood in one lifetime through tantra, as compared to the many aeons of effort required through Hinayana and the sutra level Mahayana practice. The different tantric Buddhist lineages are based on which tantras one has studied, and with which teachers one learned.

Tibetan medicine and astrology are also presented in scriptures called tantras. See also *Vajrayana.*

Tantrayana See *Vajrayana.*

ten non-virtuous actions The first three are related to actions of the body: (1) killing; (2) stealing or taking what is not freely given; (3) sexual misconduct or harmful sexual relations. The next four are related to speech: (4) lying; (5) slander or divisive speech; (6) harsh speech; (7) gossip or idle chatter. The last three are related to mind: (8) covetousness or greed; (9) anger, ill-will or hatred; (10) wrong view. The last three are synonymous with the "three poisons": desire, aversion, and ignorance. These three are the foundations of all our non-virtuous actions, through which we produce negative karma which binds us to suffering in samsara.

terma Hidden treasures. Teachings, scriptures, sadhanas and sacred objects mystically cached by Padmasambhava and his Tibetan consort, Lady Yeshe Tsogyal. Termas have been discovered hidden in caves, rocks, rivers, and within walls of buildings.

Not all termas were in material form. There are also mind termas, hidden in the dimension of meditative awareness and discovered by revelation. Termas form an important part of the Nyingmapa lineage teachings.

Three Jewels The three objects of refuge are: the Buddha or awakened teacher, the Dharma or teachings, and the Sangha or community of fellow practitioners. These three form the essential basis for successful spiritual practice.

three poisons Greed, hatred or aversion, and ignorance. Buddha taught that from these three all the suffering of samsara arises.

three realms The Desire, Form, and Formless Realms.

Three Roots In addition to the Three Jewels, in Vajrayana the practitioner also takes refuge in the Three Roots: the guru as the source of all blessings, the yidam as the source of all siddhi, and the dharma protectors as the source of enlightened activity.

three thousand world systems In Buddhist cosmology the number of world systems throughout the universe is one thousand cubed, or one billion.

Three Vehicles The Hinayana or Small Vehicle, the Mahayana or Great Vehicle, and the Vajrayana or Diamond Vehicle.

torma A ritual offering cake made of tsampa (roasted barley flour) and butter, and presented as an offering to deities and Dharma protectors. There are simple and elaborate tormas, some painted and some plain, with varied shapes and designs depending on their purpose.

transformation chakra This is the navel chakra (nirmana-chakra in Sanskrit) and is the source of creative power. Tummo practice is cented at the navel chakra, the center of creative spiritual force through which one can achieve tremendous realization. The navel chakra is also the easiest door through which to bring the energy-winds from the rest of the body into the central channel.

trikaya The three bodies of a Buddha: the nirmanakaya, the sambhogakaya, and the dharmakaya. They correlate, respectively, to the body, speech, and mind aspects of Buddha.

tsampa Roasted barley flour, a staple food of Tibetans.

tulku Incarnate lamas who have voluntarily taken human birth in fulfillment of their bodhisattva vows to help beings. The power to determine one's rebirth is gained upon attainment of the eighth stage of a bodhisattva.

tummo Inner heat yoga. The tummo practice is the first of the Six Yogas of Naropa, and serves as the foundation for all of the other yogas.

twelve links of interdependent origination These "twelve nidanas" describe the nature of samsara as well as its cause. The twelve nidanas are: (1) fundamental ignorance, (2) karmic formations or impulsive accumulations, (3) [dualistic] consciousness, (4) name and form, (5) sense consciousness, (6) contact with the phenomenal world, (7) sensation or feeling, (8) craving [for experience], (9) grasping, (10) becoming, (11) birth, (12) aging and death.

two stages of yoga The generation and completion stages of tantric meditation.

upasaka A lay Buddhist who has taken one or more of the five lay precepts.

upward moving energy-wind One of the five pranas, controlling speech and respiration.

ushnisha The mound atop a Buddha's head, forming one of the major marks of a Buddha.

vajra Indestructible, diamond-like, adamantine, thunder bolt. A ritual scepter, called "dorje" in Tibetan, used in Vajrayana practice. It symbolizes skillful means and compassion, the masculine aspect of enlightened activity. The vajra is diamond-like in that it is priceless, indestructible, and clear, symbolizing the qualities of that which is unborn and undying. It is a symbol of the power of highest truth.

Vajra Black Line Hell A hell realm where black lines are drawn on the victims' bodies and they are then cut along these lines. The Vajra Hells are the worst of the hot hell realms.

vajra body This refers to the subtle body, composed of nadis, prana, and bindu. It can also refer to the combination of the physical and subtle body in their perfected natural state.

vajracharya A vajra master, an accomplished master of both the theory and practice of Vajrayana teachings.

Vajradhara Holder of the Vajra. Vajradhara symbolizes the primordial state of the dharmakaya. Blue in color, Vajradhara is depicted wearing the ornaments of a sambhogakaya Buddha, holding a vajra in his right hand and a bell in his left hand. It is said that the Kagyu tradition was transmitted by Vajradhara to Tilopa in a vision.

Vajravarahi Diamond Sow. One of the forms of Vajrayogini, the dakini consort of Chakrasamvara. Red in color, she has a small sow's head over her ear, representing the Buddha family of Vairochana, and the transformation of ignorance and passion into dharmadhatu wisdom and compassion.

Vajrayana Diamond Vehicle, also called Mantrayana or Tantrayana. A branch of Mahayana Buddhism that first began to emerge in India, particularly in the northwestern state of Oddiyana, between the first and sixth centuries C.E. Vajrayana embraced the Mahayana ideals, but was traditionally practiced in secret. It is often referred to as the "path of transformation," as the tantric meditator trains to transform his view of ordinary reality into the extraordinary and sacred insight and perception of a Buddha.

Another hallmark of Vajrayana practice is its extensive use of visualization and ritual meditation, and the techniques of mantra, mudra, and samadhi within the context of deity yoga. Even though one is not yet enlightened, one emulates the body, speech, and mind of an enlightened deity. Thus Vajrayana is also called the "path of fruition or result," because it uses yogas that bring future results into the current practice.

Vajrayogini A semi-wrathful female yidam. Red in color, with one face and two arms, she holds an upraised hooked knife in her right hand and a skull cup full of blood in her left hand. She wears a skull crown and bone ornaments. Her symbolic meaning is the same as Vajravarahi. In some traditions, particularly the Kagyu, she is usually the first yidam used, as an introduction to the practice of Highest Yoga Tantra.

Vinaya One of the "Three Baskets" (Tripitaka) of the Buddhist scriptures, the Vinaya deals with Buddhist ethics and rules of conduct governing the life of the sangha. The bulk of the Vinaya pertains to monks and nuns, but it also contains precepts, teachings, and advice for laypeople.

vipashyana Insight. After calming and clearing the mind through shamatha meditation, the yogin will begin to have insight into the nature of mind, phenomena, and emptiness. There are progressive levels of insight meditation leading ultimately to the perfection of wisdom. While there is a systematic series of analytical meditations, as well as questions similar to Zen koans, the goal is not simply to gain an intellectual understanding of mind, but rather for the yogi to clearly realize the true nature of mind experientially.

yantra yoga A series of highly esoteric bodily movements, similar to hatha yoga, that are traditionally introduced to advanced practitioners as a preliminary exercise and a support for tummo practice. When doing intensive method path practices such as tummo, wherein the yogi is manipulating the breathing and vigorously redirecting the flow of prana in the body, obstructions in energy can easily occur. These blockages can cause serious physical, energetic, and mental problems for the yogi, as illustrated by Gampopa's experiences with Milarepa. Therefore it is important to support any energy practices with yogic movements that help to rebalance the prana and to keep the nadis supple and clear of obstacles.

Yantra is used as an aid to developing the natural state of body, breath (prana), and mind. The natural state of the mind is dependent upon establishing the natural state of prana, and the natural state of prana is founded on the natural healthy state of the vajra body. Thus yantra yoga also provides a preliminary foundation for the spontaneous presence of Mahamudra.

yidam The personal meditation deity of a Vajrayana practitioner. Although some yidams are prescribed and taught to everyone within a particular lineage at a preliminary level, the guru will later select a specific yidam for each practitioner in accordance with one's characteristic expression of Buddha nature.

As a preliminary to yidam practice, the yogi must be accomplished in guru yoga and have great faith and devotion in the guru. This enables the practitioner to identify with the lineage and to establish a deep inner connection with the yidam. In this way one can transform the energy of one's neurosis into its enlightened expression, as represented in the yidam. Identification with the yidam also cuts through deeply entrenched attachment to one's physical form.

yoga Union. The practices of Vajrayana, through which one awakens to one's innate union with the unborn nature of ultimate wisdom. Some yogas emphasize working with the body, as in yantra yoga and prostrations; others emphasize the breath, as with mantra and pranayama practice; others emphasize the mind, as in quiet seated meditation. However, none emphasize one part to the exclusion of the others; each yoga serves to train all three components of body, breath, and mind, to bring the yogi to full realization of the true nature of existence.

yogi; yogin A male yoga practitioner. In Tibet, the term yogi is often used to contrast a lay practitioner from an ordained monk. Also, since yogi can sometimes mean someone who is practicing the higher yogas, which ultimately involve taking on a sexual consort, the term yogi was often used to designate married lamas and practitioners, in contrast to celibate monks. In its general sense, however, a yogi is anyone who practices yoga, so a monk can also be called a yogi.

yogini A female yoga practitioner.

Bibliography

Burtt, E.A., *The Teachings of the Compassionate Buddha*. New York: New American Library, 1955.

Chang, Garma C. C., *The Hundred Thousand Songs of Milarepa*. New Hyde Park: University Books, 1962.

--------, *Teachings of Tibetan Yoga*. New Hyde Park: University Books, 1963.

Chogyam Trungpa Rinpoche, *Visual Dharma: The Buddhist Art of Tibet*. Berkeley & London: Shambhala Publications, 1975.

--------, "The Wheel of Life: Illusion's Game," *Garuda* (spring 1972).

Chokyi Nyima Rinpoche, *The Union of Mahamudra and Dzogchen*. Edited by Marcia B. Schmidt. Hong Kong: Rangjung Yeshe Publications, 1989.

Crystal Mirror VI. Berkeley: Dharma Publishing, 1984.

Dowman, Keith, *Masters of Mahamudra*. Albany: State University of New York Press, 1985.

--------, *Sky Dancer: The Secret Life and Songs of the Lady Yeshe Tsogyel*. London: Routledge and Kegan Paul, 1984.

Eliade, Mircea, *Yoga: Immortality and Freedom*. New York: Bollingen Pantheon, 1958.

Evans-Wentz, W.Y., *Tibetan Yoga and Secret Doctrines*. London: Oxford University Press, 1935.

--------, *Tibet's Great Yogi, Milarepa*. London: Oxford University Press, 1951.

Gampopa, *The Jewel Ornament of Liberation*. Translated by Herbert V. Guenther. Berkeley: Shambhala Publications, 1959.

Gyaltsen, Khenpo Könchog, *Prayer Flags: The Life and Spiritual Songs of Jigten Sumgon*. Ithaca: Snow Lion, 1986.

--------, *The Great Kagyu Masters*. Ithaca: Snow Lion, 1990.

Gyamtso, Khenpo Tsultrim, *Progressive Stages of Meditation on Emptiness*. Oxford: Longchen Foundation, 1986.

Gyatso, Geshe Kelsang, *Clear Light of Bliss*. London: Wisdom Publications, 1982.

Hopkins, Jeffrey, *Compassion in Tibetan Buddhism*. London: Rider, 1980.

Jigme Gyalway Nyugu Paltrul Rinpoche, *Kun-zang La-may Zhal-lung*. Vol. 4. Upper Montclair: Diamond-Lotus Publishing, 1989.

Kalsang, Lama Thubten, *Atisha*. New Delhi: Mahayana Publications, 1974.

Kalu Rinpoche, *The Dharma That Illuminates All Beings Impartially Like the Light of the Sun and Moon*. Albany: State University of New York Press, 1986.

--------, *The Gem Ornament of Manifold Oral Instructions Which Benefits Each and Everyone Appropriately*. San Francisco: KSK Publications, 1986.

Khetsun Sangpo Rinbochay, *Tantric Practice in Nyingma*. Ithaca: Gabriel Snow Lion, 1982.

Lati Rinbochay, Denma Locho Rinbochay, Leah Zahler, and Jeffrey Hopkins, *Meditative States in Tibetan Buddhism*. London: Wisdom Publications, 1983.

Lhalungpa, Lobsang P., *The Life of Milarepa*. Boulder: Prajna Press, 1982.

MacDonald, Kathleen, *How to Meditate*. Boston: Wisdom Publications, 1984.

Mullin, Glenn H., *Selected Works of the Dalai Lama II: The Tantric Yogas of Sister Niguma*. Ithaca: Snow Lion, 1982.

Nalanda Translation Committee and Chogyam Trungpa, *The Rain of Wisdom*. Boulder: Shambhala, 1980.

--------, *The Life of Marpa the Translator*. Boulder: Prajna Press, 1982.

Namgyal, Takpo Tashi, *Mahamudra: The Quintessence of Mind and Meditation*. Translated by Lobsang P. Lhalungpa. Boston & London: Shambhala, 1986.

Norbu, Namkhai, *Dream Yoga and the Practice of Natural Light*. Ithaca: Snow Lion, 1992.

--------, *The Dzogchen Ritual Practices*. Edited and translated by Brian Beresford. London: Kailash Editions, 1991.

--------, *Yantra Yoga: Yoga of Movements*. Edited by Oliver F. Leick. Gleisdorf: Tsaparang, 1988.

Piburn, Sidney, ed., *The Dalai Lama: A Policy of Kindness*. Ithaca: Snow Lion, 1990.

Rhie, Marilyn, and Robert A.F. Thurman, *Wisdom and Compassion: The Sacred Art of Tibet*. New York: Asian Art Museum of San Francisco and Tibet House New York, in association with Harry N. Abrams Publishers, 1991.

Schmid, Toni, *The Cotton-Clad Mila: The Tibetan Poet-Saint's Life in Pictures*. Stockholm: Statens Etnografiska Museum, 1952.

Shantideva, *A Guide to the Bodhisattva's Way of Life*. Translated by Stephen Batchelor. Dharamsala: Library of Tibetan Works and Archives, 1979

Thaye, Jampa, *A Garland of Gold: The Early Kagyu Masters in India and Tibet*. Bristol: Ganesha Press, 1990.

Thinley, Karma, *The History of the Sixteen Karmapas of Tibet*. Boulder: Prajna Press, 1980.

Thrangu Rinpoche, *Showing the Path to Liberation*. Manila: Tara Publishing, 1983.

Tulku Thondup, *Enlightened Living: Teachings of Tibetan Buddhist Masters*. Boston & London: Shambhala, 1990.

Tulku Urgyen Rinpoche, *Repeating the Words of the Buddha*. Kathmandu: Rangjung Yeshe Publications, 1991.

Waddell, L. Austine, *Tibetan Buddhism*. New York: Dover, 1972.

INDEX

Printed in the United States
by Baker & Taylor Publisher Services